EWAN McGREGOR

Laura Jackson

EWAN McGREGOR

A FORCE

TO BE

RECKONED

WITH

All best
Laura Jackson

PIATKUS

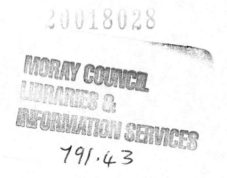
This is an unauthorised biography.
None of the individuals referred to have endorsed or in any way sponsored this book.

First published in 1999 by
Judy Piatkus (Publishers) Ltd
5 Windmill Street
London W1P 1HF

The moral rights of the author have been asserted

A catalogue record for this book is available from the British Library

ISBN 0-7499-1939-6

Text design by Paul Saunders

Typeset by Phoenix Photosetting, Chatham, Kent
Printed and bound in Great Britain by Butler & Tanner Ltd, Frome, Somerset

Contents

Dedicated to my very special husband, David

Acknowledgements

Grateful appreciation to everyone whom I interviewed for this book. My thanks for all contributions to: Rosalind Anderson; Kenny Baker; David Bannerman; Janet Betts; Isla Blair; Ted Childs; Malcolm Clegg; Matthew Cooper; Fred Feast; Nicky Franklin; Peter Haig; Roy Hudd; Jonathan Hyde; Philip Jackson; Stratford Johns; Chris Kelly; Peter Martin; Barry Norman CBE; Joseph O'Conor; Otto Plaschkes; Alan Plater; Carl Prechezer; Lord David Puttnam; Natasha Ross; Robin Soans; Jon Snow; Bob Stewart; Revd Henry Tait; Rosemarie Whitman;

Also thanks for their help to: Bafta; Bafta Scotland; BBC TV; BBC Radio Times (Anna); BBC World Service (Joanne Hopper); BBC Written Archives (Neil Somerville); British Society of Cinematographers; Central TV; Channel 4 TV; Mark Chambers, Colin Black and Grant Cobban, (Bissett & Taylor); Compulsive Viewing (Madeleine French); Elgin Library staff; Glasgow Film Fund (Judy Anderson); Grampian TV (Bill Moir and Hilary Buchan); Grimethorpe Social Club; Irish Film Board; *Irish Times*; *New York Times*; Perth Library; Perth Theatre; Salisbury Playhouse (Arthur Millie); *Scarborough Evening News* (Margaret); *Scottish Screen*, Glasgow; *Sight and Sound*; Skreba Films; Society of Cinematographers, Paris; *Spotlight*; *The Express*; *The Face*; *The Independent*; *The List* (Alan Morrison); *Time Out*; Unique Pictures, Elgin. Special thanks to David for his unending help and encouragement, and also thanks to my editor Rachel Winning and all at Piatkus Books.

'Ewan McGregor is one of the very best young actors of his generation. He is more talented than his American counterparts – the likes of Leonardo DiCaprio and Brad Pitt.'

BARRY NORMAN

CHAPTER 1

An Actor's Life
For Me

B Y THE AGE of just twenty-eight, Ewan McGregor had been dubbed 'the jammiest actor in Britain'. And with good reason. Yet to claim good luck alone has been responsible for his phenomenal rise to stardom and international pin-up status would be to do him a disservice. Not only is he one of the busiest young actors in the industry, but the trajectory of his career has been truly meteoric.

In ten short years, since leaving school armed with nothing but a passionate desire to see himself on the silver screen, Ewan McGregor sprinted through three years of training, leaving drama school six months early to chalk up the first of two lead roles in major television serials, and went on to appear in over a dozen movies. In his heart there was never any confusion, no soul-searching: he had known with complete certainty from the age of nine exactly where he was headed, even if those around him had still to be convinced. And from landing that first role, with the unrelenting single-mindedness of a guided missile, he has consistently continued to defy one of the cardinal rules of acting: that the first thing an actor must learn to accept is rejection.

Instead he carved his own unique route, forging relentlessly on, nailing his breakthrough role in the 1994 cult film *Shallow Grave* before springboarding onto the world cinematic stage – and achieving instant junkie icon status – as Mark Renton, the anti-hero in the controversial and breathtakingly hard-hitting 1996 drug-culture movie *Trainspotting*. McGregor's shaven-headed, tormented face and emaciated frame would launch a thousand trips. His personal journey might be said to culminate in him landing the biggest role of his life: the coveted lead as the fabled Jedi knight Obi-Wan Kenobi in all three of George Lucas's new *Star Wars* series, commencing in 1999 with *Star Wars Episode One: The Phantom Menace*, the first of the three-part prequel to the original trilogy and a movie variously described as 'The movie event of the millennium' and 'The most anticipated film in movie history'.

Such startling and rapid success comes as no surprise to those who have encountered the vibrant dynamism of Ewan McGregor's personality and the style with which he attacks life and work. Oscar-winning film producer Lord David Puttnam was one of the earliest to spot McGregor's screen worth when the young actor made his film debut in the Warner Brothers' 1993 film *Being Human*. It was the smallest of bit parts, yet it gave McGregor sufficient scope for Puttnam to note, 'The camera loves him.' And the most respected movie critic on British television, Barry Norman, with all his experience of watching film stars down the years, is categorical. 'Ewan McGregor is one of the very best young actors of his generation. He is more talented than his American counterparts – the likes of Leonardo DiCaprio and Brad Pitt.'

But perhaps most crucially, the person with the most faith in Ewan McGregor has always been McGregor himself. Whilst acknowledging that his fame at times feels like a fairytale, his bold self-confidence is characteristic. 'I was always driven to go as far as I could. I was always very arrogant about it and I never ever imagined it any other way. I never considered the alternative.'

The roots of this confidence undoubtedly lie in the charmed path of his personal as well as his professional life. He may have acquired, among his varied accolades, a reputation as the outwardly aggressive-looking 'Face of the Nineties', but in reality he brims with enthusiasm and exudes infectious humour. He is also refreshingly devoid of the stereotypical mass of Nineties' hang-ups: no hateful parents to blame for secret sorrows, no wrong-side-of-the-tracks upbringing to resent. And whereas a celebrity family connection can have its drawbacks, his stage and screen actor uncle Denis Lawson, of *Local Hero* fame, is someone of whom McGregor is fiercely proud. Indeed his mother's colourfully renegade younger brother was the early inspiration for the lively young boy in every sense. Like his uncle, Ewan yearned to be different – not something easily achieved, considering, geographically, where it all began.

He was born Ewan Gordon McGregor in the evening of 31 March 1971 at the Royal Infirmary in Perth, Scotland, the second son of James and Carol McGregor. His clear blue eyes made an arresting contrast to his reddish hair. From the moment his proud parents took him home to meet his two-year-old brother Colin, he proved to be a bright spark.

Home was Edgemont, a house in Sauchie Terrace in Crieff, a well-to-do holiday resort since Victorian times. Romantically tagged 'the gateway to the Highlands', the town is located picturesquely in the centre of Scotland. McGregor's first five years were spent playing around this quiet cul-de-sac close to parks, playing fields and the local cemetery, with the River Earn flowing by behind. By all accounts he was an adventurous boy growing up in a happy, secure and close-knit community, and cherished by his doting parents. He was a cheery child with a mobile face and a winning smile.

What lay behind that smile, however, even at this early stage, was a rapidly developing and highly fertile mind. His most noticeable trait was a capacity for relentless determination – a determination which first revealed itself when he took his initial, albeit unwitting, steps towards his future career at the tender age of six.

It was a church production staged by Reverend Henry Tait, the minister of Crieff's South Church. He had cast McGregor in the central role: an ambitious choice considering that there was one significant snag. The boy could not yet read. But the young McGregor refused to be thwarted. With the kind of tenacity with which he would later become associated, he learned his lines parrot-fashion, endlessly repeating them as his mother patiently read them out to him over and over again each night at home. Practice made perfect and by the time rehearsals came around McGregor was raring to go – as the minister vividly recalls.

'Unlike most children Ewan didn't need coaxing. I wanted a New Testament story interspersed with Old Testament episodes . . . That year the story was to be David and Goliath. We had a large Sunday School, large enough to put together two armies – the Philistines and the Israelites. In the part of Goliath we cast a tall lad with a spear and eventually out comes this tiny child with his sling and lops Goliath's head off. Ewan was the small child – David.'

The play was not a wild success but Reverend Tait remembers, 'In my diary I recorded that 'wee Ewan McGregor was wonderful'. Of course it ran in the family. His uncle Denis Lawson was in my Youth Fellowship thirty-odd years ago. But I firmly believed that this child was obviously a little actor and would be recognised as such. He was surely a natural.'

Whether or not McGregor himself was aware of any green shoots of aptitude, his interest in acting was already grounded by having an uncle who, when he visited his sister and her family, brought a dash of exotic colour into the tartan, tweedy, and deeply conservative confines of Crieff. Denis Lawson – thirty years old in 1977, dark-haired and handsome – already had an established track record on the London stage and was busy breaking into the wider realms of television and film. He was also a refugee from the glorious Swinging Sixties and still dressed the part, judging by McGregor's earliest recollections of his flamboyant relative. As he is fond of recounting about his uncle, 'He was an extraordinary character! There were a lot of tweedy people in Crieff, farmers and stuff, and my uncle would arrive with long hair, wearing a sheepskin waistcoat, beads and no shoes and he would give people flowers. I'd go . . . "Who is this man?" He fascinated me.'

The joy of these memorable visits was further intensified by the interaction between uncle and nephew on a deeper level as, over the years, together they would work out theatrical routines. McGregor unashamedly idolised Denis Lawson to such a degree that it would have been astonishing had he *not* been drawn to a profession which allowed, even encouraged, such anarchic self-expression. His own future attraction to film would crystallise when, along with his parents and brother, he went to the cinema super-charged with excitement at the prospect of seeing his uncle up on the wide screen.

The film was the 1977 Twentieth Century Fox blockbuster *Star Wars*. Directed by George Lucas and based on a blend of influences including the old Flash Gordon and Buck Rogers television serials with a splash of chivalrous knights of old thrown in, it starred Mark Hamill, Harrison Ford and Carrie Fisher. Roughly half of the $11 million budget had been spent to spectacular effect on futuristic sets and a host of amazing special effects.

Denis Lawson's role was as Wedge, an X-wing fighter pilot involved in an inter-galactic good-versus-evil fight at the end of the film. The impact on McGregor of watching his uncle along with the rest of the stunned cinema-goers was profound. 'This was the first time I'd been to the cinema to see my uncle Denis in a movie and I thought that that was about the most exciting thing that had ever happened in my life. It was kind of a double whammy. The movie threw me – and so did he.'

The whole *Star Wars* phenomenon made an incredible impression on the world's youngsters. Like millions of other kids McGregor could not get it out of his head. At play he improvised with toy light-sabres and he was such an avid fan of the film that he became near word-perfect at reciting its dialogue. He would while away hours happily wrapped up in a make-believe world. The experience opened up whole new vistas to him, including his first awareness of the female sex. Carrie Fisher had played the heroine Princess Leia in a white ankle-length gown with long loose sleeves and her hair set in coils over her ears; she provided glamour but also fought alongside the men and, when impersonating the film's characters with his friends, McGregor often opted to play her. As he later revealed, 'Princess Leia was probably my first serious crush.'

But despite this latest passion and the theatrical family connection, the predominant influences in the home were scholastic. His mother Carol was a teacher at the local high school (she later became deputy head teacher at the King's Park special school in Dundee), while his father Jim taught physical education at Crieff's Morrison's Academy. Established in 1860 and with a reputation for sound traditional teaching methods, co-educational independent Morrison's Academy in Ferntower Road took pupils aged from five to eighteen years on a fee-paying basis. It was a boarding school but also accepted day pupils and, because Jim taught there, both the McGregor boys were granted a special deal to attend. Today, Ewan appears defensive when reminded about his public-school past. 'It wasn't that posh,' he is quick to retort. 'We didn't have our own language or anything.'

In class he was bright enough – he would leave with four O levels – but he had no desire to apply himself academically, an attitude which frustrated teachers and his parents alike. In the playground he tried to be all things to all people; because he has confessed, 'of an incredible desire to be loved and wanted.' He added, 'Which is also a lot to do with acting – "Please like me! Oh fucking *please, everybody* like me!"' Inevitably his attempts failed. Talking of his inability to become a convincing schoolboy tough he says, 'I would've liked to have been. I was always trying to get into all the different cliques, trying to be part of them all, not being one or the other. That kind of sums me up, I think.'

The one area in which his singlemindedness set him aside was his love of films. He enjoyed the usual rough and tumble of growing up, playing commando games with his mates and generally allowing his high spirits to get him into mischief – to the point that his youthful exuberance once pitched him head-first off his bike and into hospital for two days suffering from concussion. But as the years unfolded his attraction to the world of cinema refined itself almost daily until, by the age of eight, he was irresistibly drawn to watching an endless stream of old movies. Instead of going out to play with his friends at weekends, he was often to be found sprawled on the lounge carpet in front of the television, absorbed in a succession of Hollywood and Ealing Studios classics. By his own later admission he was a sucker for love stories: 'If it was black and white and romantic, it was good enough for me.' Frank Capra's RKO 1946 comedy-drama *It's A Wonderful Life*, as well as his later fantasy, *Harvey*, featured at the top of his list and both starred his favourite actor, the charming and ponderous American James Stewart.

What would have been a passing phase in other children had by now become clearly defined in McGregor's head. He finds no difficulty in pinpointing the moment when his 'hobby' took on significance. 'I was going to be an actor since I was nine. I didn't know what that meant. I didn't know it meant pretending to be another person. I suppose I thought about it in terms of being like one of the people in those films. But from then on everything was geared towards it.'

At nine he had also arrived at the related conclusion that he wanted to be *different*. To stand out from the crowd. This desire was not purely sparked by the influence of his uncle, strong though that was. It was something he felt deep within himself; what Denis Lawson did was show him the way. And his passion, once recognised, was to find a focus surprisingly early. His earlier crush on Princess Leia had sown the seeds of his fascination with acting on an acutely sensual level. He makes no secret of

The Glasgow Film Theat
Seat Dedication Scheme

Honorary Patron
Ewan McGregor

PREVIOUS PAGE As Honorary Patron, Ewan takes time out to present an award as part of the Glasgow Film Theatre seat dedication scheme.

RIGHT A 15-year-old Ewan makes his television debut playing the French Horn in the Grampian Television series *A Touch of Music*.

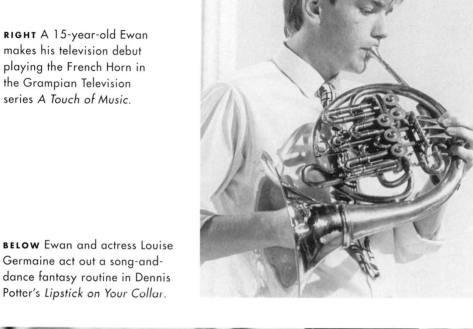

BELOW Ewan and actress Louise Germaine act out a song-and-dance fantasy routine in Dennis Potter's *Lipstick on Your Collar*.

his unadulterated joy in being an actor – and where a good part of that joy lies. As he once explained, 'A major reason for loving acting is that, even as a kid, I felt it was a very sexy profession. For me it all started in the theatre. I used to go to pantomimes as a kid and women would always play the guy and the guys would play the girls. The women who played guys would all wear these sexy fishnet stockings and I was obsessed with actresses' legs from the first pantomine I saw. I always felt very sexy when I was in the theatre. I fell in love with actresses all the time.'

From the age of about twelve or thirteen he began talking openly and frequently of his intention to become an actor. Crucially, from an academic point of view, what interest he had had in school steadily began to diminish; they were teaching him nothing about the only way of life he cared about. Over time this withdrawal became pronounced. 'I wasn't rebellious,' McGregor says. 'I didn't burn things down or break things but I was having a hard time with some of my teachers.' For a while it was a regular occurrence for him to be frogmarched to the deputy headmaster's office. Luckily the man was understanding of this precocious pupil and potential punishment evaporated into a good laugh. 'I got on with the guy,' McGregor remembers. 'We had a few great chats together.'

But, despite McGregor's craving for the theatrical limelight, he was not tempted to start honing his talents by taking part in amateur productions. According to him, 'I was always quite arrogant, and didn't want to do it until I could do it properly, so I avoided school plays.' His refusal, however, was not absolute. Whilst at Morrison's he did take the romantic lead in a production of *Sganarelle*, a Molière farce, but his commitment to the play was so far from being amateur that he relentlessly quizzed the drama teacher about what was expected of him.

He was, though, by no means obsessed with acting to the exclusion of all else. He had many creative leanings and, as he grew up, learned to express these. He took Scottish country dancing lessons; learned to play the French horn; and he also played drums in his school's pipe band. It was discovered, too, that he had a well-modulated singing voice. He also learned to ride at the riding school attached to the town's renowned Crieff Hydro Hotel. All these pursuits made for an energetic and varied early life, as well as laying the rudiments of the skills that he would later employ as a versatile actor.

By the time he was fifteen, Ewan was developing skills in other areas. His love of music and art had been greatly stifled at school, where pupils are routinely straitjacketed into largely academic activities. To compensate he joined a rock band. He became the drummer for a school band called Scarlet Pride. He certainly looked the part, having already taken to streaking his now trendy spiked hairstyle with red poster paint. In childhood Ewan had been a big fan of Elvis Presley; having been born at the outbreak of glam rock he was too young to take any interest in the psychedelic Seventies or in the short-lived but influential punk rock era. By 1986, though, his ritual each morning before leaving for school involved listening to Billy Idol who, having gone solo five years before, had mutated from raw punk into the more mainstream New Wave. His album *Rebel Yell* howled repeatedly from a bedroom window of the McGregor household at this time. After school, in teenage tradition, he took to the sanctuary of his bedroom where, on a couple of occasions, he tried his hand at songwriting. One wall was dominated by a poster of his childhood favourite Elvis Presley. His two Madonna calendars, however, remained out of sight in a drawer. She just wasn't cool enough for the rebellious McGregor.

His new wild look, coupled with the status of playing in a rock band, went hand in hand with his by now well developed penchant for swearing. 'I like swearing,' he declares with a grin, recounting how at fourteen he was thrown off a golf course for his loud and frequent bad language. 'After every shot,' he explains, 'I'd get really angry, screaming, "Fuck!" Eventually this guy drove up in a tractor and told me I had to leave. I walked back to the clubhouse all on my own in shame.'

By this stage there was not much that was shy and retiring about the adolescent McGregor. He had natural charm and his physical appeal had been steadily strengthening to match it. Of average height and build, he nevertheless exuded sexual vibrancy, with a broad smile that could by turns be cherubic and roguish. The impudent glint of self-confidence provided an added dimension to pale blue eyes already sharp with the light of his old ally: determination.

McGregor had swiftly graduated from the days when he and his mates would lurk in The Knock – a wooded area on the outskirts of Crieff –

and bounce fir cones harmlessly but annoyingly off unsuspecting girls riding by on horseback. He had progressed as far as the girls were concerned to kisses and cuddles – his favourite venue for such exploratory advances unsurprisingly proving to be the local cinema, deserted in daytime. It was no more than the grope-and-grapple stage, but he was bold with it. His outgoing personality and unusual sense of purpose made him, by accident or design, a magnet to a string of teenage girls. According to Vicky McNally, who at sixteen became his steady girlfriend, 'all the girls were after him'.

McGregor was serious enough about the relationship to spend his time in class writing her a steady stream of love notes. Outside school he would join his friends at a nearby hotel to indulge in the usual under-age drinking as well as smoking. McNally was not a smoker or a drinker but one day she was tempted to take an experimental draw of a friend's cigarette. McGregor happened upon them at exactly that moment. Although he smoked himself, he flew into a temper at what he had caught sight of and stormed off. Not long after this the couple split up.

This level of touchiness was unusual: his mates remember him as the perennial joker, always game for a laugh. The fact that this playfulness spilled over into the classroom did nothing to appease his already irked teachers; neither did it reflect any enjoyment of school on McGregor's part. By now he swung from supreme indifference to studies to a burning desire to get away. He could not have made a sharper contrast to his elder brother Colin, who was a brilliant sportsman and an impressive scholar, as well as being school captain and head boy to boot. (Colin would go on to become a Royal Air Force Tornado pilot.) While both Jim and Carol McGregor hoped that their younger son would emulate Colin's achievements, neither of them put him under any form of real pressure. In the liberal and supportive atmosphere at home they were ultimately prepared to encourage him in whichever direction he chose. Nevertheless, McGregor *was* conscious of having something to live up to.

Speaking of his brother and of his own final phase at school he recalls, 'Colin and a group of prefects were the ones chosen to tell other pupils to get out of buildings at lunch time. They were kind of like a mini Gestapo. They got to wear different colour ties and all that. I started my last year of school the year he had just finished being head boy. It was hard for me and I just couldn't hack it any more.' Teachers considered that he had had an attitude problem; he has since partly accepted this as true, but his overall verdict on the supposed best years of his life is typically frank. 'I didn't hate school. I just didn't get it.'

He did not think, however, that his parents would countenance his leaving, although at age sixteen he was, in Scotland, legally entitled to quit school if he wanted. So his mother's words came as a complete shock to him. 'After six weeks of my staying on for my last year I was driving into Crieff with my mum and it was pouring with rain. I remember the windscreen wipers were smacking about and she turned to me and said, "Listen, I've spoken to your father and if you want to leave school then you can, if you like." I'd just imagined I'd have to go through two more years of school. I never imagined that I could leave and I said, "Right. I'll leave!" '

In October 1987 McGregor left Morrison's Academy for the last time. Whilst deeply grateful to his parents for having recognised and accepted his needs, he quickly found that his relief at leaving what he saw as the pointless drudgery of school life behind was overlaid by a new, natural and profound emotion – fear. Fear of stepping out into the unknown without any guarantees of what would happen in the future. 'It was quite scary,' he admits, but the feeling did not last long. He tackled it as he did all else – head on – and within a week he had landed his first job; one, moreover, that set his restless feet firmly on his chosen path. From that point on, he would never look back.

CHAPTER 2

Tunnel Vision

T CAME AS no surprise to anyone connected with Perth Theatre that it was McGregor's first port of call when looking for work. He had been badgering them with regular telephone calls and letters since he was fourteen, begging to be allowed to do something – anything. This time when he rang he got the answer he longed for. The repertory company were looking for extras for a production of E M Forster's *A Passage To India* and he was welcome to come along.

The part required nothing more challenging than 'running around in a turban', as he put it, but he was thrilled none the less. More important, he promptly managed to get his foot in the door by talking his way into working backstage as a £50-a-week scene shifter. 'I never actually acted on that stage,' admitted McGregor later. 'I was a very humble stagehand. But I did learn a lot from watching what the other actors did. That's often the best way to gain experience.'

He could hardly have chosen a better first hunting ground. Perth Theatre enjoyed a well-deserved reputation for fostering a wealth of talent and providing a stepping stone for a whole galaxy of future stars of the stage and screen. But when asked if he had been drawn there by its good name, McGregor irreverently rapped back, 'Nah. It was just the nearest.' But such cynicism belied the wide-eyed wonder with which he entered into this new and stimulating period of his life.

Although elegant and prosperous Perth was indeed only a few miles from his home town, it was McGregor's first taste of something approaching cosmopolitan city life. He recalls, 'Those first six months were amazing. Suddenly I was in the theatre, learning about discipline. I met all kinds of people for the first time. I met gay people and I met people who were having affairs. It was such a different and exciting world compared to the very tiny conservative town I came from.'

His break from that tiny town was not, of course, as yet complete. At sixteen he still lived at home and travelled back and forth between Crieff and Perth daily by car. But he quickly found an acute sense of belonging. 'I felt that I had made the right decision in leaving school. I felt that the theatre was my school and that I should have been there my whole schooling life.'

It has to be said that the intensity of the theatre company's newest and most exhaustively willing recruit may at times have become distinctly wearing. McGregor himself freely owns up to the fact that initially he got under everybody's feet – and on a few people's nerves. 'I was such a pain because I was so keen and I wanted to do this and that. They were all so fed up with me and my dreams. But they stuck me out and by the end of it I came out a much more mature person. After that I was ready for my formal training as an actor.'

That formal training began to take shape when, in the spring of 1988, he signed up for a one-year foundation course in drama at Kirkcaldy College of Technology. There he threw himself into long days of study as well as painting scenery and taking part in student productions with varying degrees of success. By now he had struck his first blow for real independence by leaving home and moving in to the college's halls of residence. For the next twelve months he set about spreading his wings, indulging in the usual student pursuits and keeping up an impressive round of socialising, haunting the local pubs and nightclubs.

Until now his relationships with girls had been casual; it was only now, when he was in Kirkcaldy, that he broadened this particular horizon. On the surface he appeared confident and assured but his bravado masked a sensitivity to the whole issue of losing his virginity. When the moment did arrive it was, he would later recall, memorable. In an area where experience counts he was clearly happy to submit to the tender mercies of the girl in question, judging by the typically frank quip he delivered when asked about it. 'I didn't know what it was about. Then somebody took hold of me and gave me a good one.' He was soon to concentrate his love interest in a fellow student called Hannah Titley who would, for the duration of his time at Kirkcaldy, become his constant companion. Hannah Titley's aim was to become a stage manager and the couple inspired and encouraged each other in their ambitions.

McGregor's focus remained steadfast; the foundation course only served to further reinforce his self-belief. 'I hadn't been mistaken all this time,' he thought, but as yet he could have no way of knowing precisely for which medium he was ultimately destined. He had, however, already had a tiny taste of seeing himself on television. Whilst still a pupil at Morrison's Academy he had been selected to take part in a Grampian Television series called *A Touch Of Music* which aimed to showcase young musical talent. McGregor's three-minute solo slot playing the French horn had been recorded in 1986 and was transmitted the following year. At fifteen years old his idea of appearing rebellious while performing Mozart had been to wipe his nose on his sleeve between passages. Capturing the appearance on video tape, his parents for years after would entertain McGregor's girlfriends with it, despite the fact that it had gone out in an edited version – as he later laughed, 'They had to keep cutting to the pianist.' That gauche performance was an age away now. Still, technically speaking, it stands as Ewan McGregor's television debut.

McGregor continued fervently to plough the furrow towards his professional acting debut. But he had a way to go yet. Indeed the nearest he got to it in 1988 was waiting on tables at an Italian restaurant in Edinburgh's Grassmarket area during the city's annual Film Festival. At Gennaro's he made his mark by flirting skilfully with the female customers.

Personally he remained game for anything, outgoing and outrageous, experimenting with hair dye, going to drastic extremes and shaving almost the whole lot off. But his larkish ability to live every day to the full didn't detract from his tunnel vision when viewing the future. He was unable to envisage himself fitting into a 'normal' way of life – and unwilling to even contemplate failure in achieving his chosen goal. Any prospective actor is forced to acknowledge that it is a notoriously difficult profession in which to succeed – there are no easy shortcuts. But rejection was an unknown concept to McGregor until, when approaching the end of his year-long course, the time came to take his next and major step by applying for a place at drama school.

The inspirational Denis Lawson had attended the Scottish Royal Academy of Dramatic Arts in Glasgow, but McGregor had his heart and sights set on heading south. Early in 1989 he therefore began applying to audition at various drama schools. His first approach was to London-based RADA – and he was turned down. The experience, so unique for him, left enough of a mark on him for him to relive it – and wreak his revenge – on UK television nine years later, as a guest on the BBC chatshow, *Parkinson*.

As McGregor vividly recalled, he had had to find the money for the train fare plus RADA's audition fee. He retold what happened next. 'So you come down and you've spent about a hundred quid and you're skint and I walked into the room and there was one guy. Surely if you're gonna test people to see if they're talented and interesting you maybe should have a couple of people, maybe three or four. But there was one man sitting behind a desk. I walked in and I was seventeen. I was gonna be eighteen by the time their year started and I was gonna get in, you know? And he went, "So, Ewan, come and sit and have a chat." I went, "Well, surely you'd like to see my speeches first." I had them all under my belt, Shakespeare and modern and everything. And he went, "No, no, come and we'll have a wee chat." He asked, "How old are you?" I said "Seventeen." He went, "Ah, well, you've got a good few years auditioning yet." I went, "Eh? What? Excuse me? I've just wedged out a hundred quid to get down here and you've written me off already!"'

McGregor had not taken kindly to the snub then and he still resented it in 1998, judging by his next reaction. To a spontaneous spurt of laughter from the studio audience, he released his own burst of fiendish amusement, declaring, 'They're sorry now – RADA!' and presented, on air, two vigorous two-fingered salutes to the prestigious Academy. At the time, RADA's summary rejection knocked him sideways. Fortunately, before he could become too demoralised, his application to the equally prestigious Guildhall School of Music and Drama in London was accepted. According to him he got in by pretending to be an elastic band; whatever, he pulled off a significant coup, for he was one of just twenty successful applicants out of over 700. He promptly signed up for a three-year course starting in the summer of 1989.

Unsurprisingly his uncle Denis had been instrumental in helping him to achieve this important goal, as McGregor, years later, would recount. 'It was Denis who helped me with my drama school audition speeches. One afternoon in the school gym he showed me what it was like to be an actor, doing a speech from Jim Cartwright's play *Road*. There's a lot of swearing and I played it as a thick-accented Scotsman, which gave it a double meaning – I'd just been beaten up in Glasgow and to get me angry enough, Denis was employing what they call "emotional recall". "Remember their faces," he kept saying, "you're not angry enough. Swear! Say motherfucker, cunt, shit." To begin with it was slightly embarrassing because he was my uncle Denis. But then suddenly it didn't matter any more. I was in a fury, spitting and screaming these swearwords and Denis was shouting, "More, more." Then the janitor burst in to see me screaming "Motherfucker!" It was the first serious acting I'd ever done – a kind of controlled loss of control which is a wonderful feeling and it was the first time I'd ever felt that. Denis showed me how to behave in another way, which is surely all that acting can ever be.'

Lawson too never forgot this moment in his young relative's life. Ewan had told Denis back when he was nine of his desire to become an actor. Lawson had replied, 'Come back in ten years' – but he had been proud all the same. 'It was thrilling that Ewan had picked up on what I was doing. When he was auditioning for drama school I suggested a couple of speeches for him and did this emotion-memory experience with him. I'm not a great believer in all that stuff but he'd had a run-in with a guy over a girl a few days before, so I got him to release his anger, which was quite impressive.

'But I'd spotted something much earlier than that. Ewan was a drummer in the school pipe band. They were having a competition in the school one evening. When it came to Ewan's turn, he played this solo and I realised that he knew exactly what he was doing – he was drawing in an audience through his concentration. Women like men when they look concentrated. It's something I'm very aware of on stage and I recognised it in Ewan immediately. It's a subtle and powerful way of transmitting sexuality. That day I thought, "Yes, this is a peformer." We politely call it stage presence. But actually it's sex.'

Leaving Scotland was the start of McGregor realising his dream, leaving Kirkcaldy meant parting company with Hannah Titley. The year they had spent together had clearly made a strong impression on him; it inspired his single, doomed attempt to try his hand at scriptwriting (the attempt quickly foundered when he found it hard to handle the dialogue): 'It was about a summer I spent in Edinburgh during the arts festival when I was with Hannah. It was a fantastic summer and I was trying to write something about that time.'

As one door quietly closed another flew open. McGregor eagerly joined the new influx of students at the Guildhall in London's Silk Street. An unpleasant surprise or two awaited him. 'I always thought I was fantastic until I got to drama school, where that notion was soundly thrashed out.' He was now only one amongst many talented young hopefuls. For the first time in his life he became self-conscious, which undermined his confidence and pricked his hitherto unassailable faith in his own ability.

As one of McGregor's tutors later explained, the sheer nature of such rigorous training will sap anyone's self-belief. Actors in particular learn very quickly to make fools of themselves in front of others. If they can accept the consequences of this, their self-belief should return in a stronger and more positive form than before.

At the Guildhall McGregor learnt a variety of traditional dramatic techniques, including mime. He did not, however, subscribe to the method style of acting favoured by the likes of fellow Briton Daniel Day-Lewis. He tended to echo the more light-hearted approach of Hollywood superstar Mel Gibson, who described the intensity of method acting as 'too much like hard work'.

But hard work, when it came to furthering his ambition, was something of which McGregor was never shy. He was straining at the leash to get on with his career. A student's first year at drama school is mainly restricted to classes and training, not all of which appear to be particularly relevant at times. On one occasion, McGregor revealed that he was expected to be a cup of coffee. Incredulously he queried, 'How do you do that? And why should it matter?' It is only in the second year that the hands-on experience of stage work can begin. For the twenty-year-old McGregor, with his good looks, this meant taking on the traditional romantic lead roles. He recalls 'a lot of young-lover acting. In my second year I played Orlando in *As You Like It* which toured to Istanbul and Hamburg. That boosted my confidence quite a lot, because I'd always been scared of Shakespeare.'

What this particular, 'respectable' role also did was convince his parents, particularly his father, that he was on the right track. His mother Carol maintains that she had always been sure that her son would succeed, but Jim McGregor had had his reservations. In his role as Morrison's Academy's career guidance officer, he was only too aware of the insecurity which infamously accompanies an acting career; he was cautious of recommending such a profession to any boy or girl, let alone his own son. Despite the fact that McGregor had been fiercely committed to this career from the age of nine, it was not until he watched his son in action in *As You Like It* that he finally arrived at the conclusion that he had what it took to be a success, even in such a competitive field.

Rapidly recovering from the previous dent in his confidence, McGregor's gimlet eyes were fixed more passionately than ever on his ultimate destination. There was a restless energy about him; he was more than willing to take risks. In the first six months of his final year he harvested as many of his talents as he could, exploring, expanding and utilising the full range of his dramatic skills. Including the ability to sing and dance.

At school, before his voice broke, McGregor had been a soloist in the choir and he had continued to develop his singing. His childhood experience of dance had been confined to the distinctive and intricate discipline of Scottish country dancing for which he had trained in his spare time. 'My mates used to give me a hard time about that,' he later confessed, 'but I couldn't help myself because I love singing and dancing.' At the Guildhall he thrived under the tuition of a wider and more varied form of dance, for which he showed natural aptitude. These talents are meant to feature among the basic tools of any actor's future trade, but for McGregor they would come into play far earlier than he had bargained for.

They were certainly put to good use when, in January 1992 the college staged an agents' evening attended by 150 casting directors and representatives from actors' agencies. For these nerve-racking events students are expected to split their showcase performance into three sections – a song-and-dance routine, a two-hander and a brief solo piece. The gut-churning importance of such an audition was not lost on McGregor, who has since bluntly described it as 'a fuckin' nightmare! Just such a huge opportunity, totally terrifying.'

When it came to his turn, on a cocktail of nerves and adrenalin he launched himself headlong through the song-and-dance routine and performed, as his two-hander, a scene from the Bruce Robinson-directed 1986 comedy *Withnail & I* (appropriately, about two out-of-work actors). Then came the third and final solo section. And McGregor thought he blew it. He had written an original piece featuring an amputee ex-rig worker in Scotland's oil capital, Aberdeen. Having propelled himself on stage in a wheelchair, midway through his dramatic discourse, to his shocked dismay, his mind suddenly went blank. Says McGregor, 'I was sitting there, frantically rubbing my stumps, trying to remember my line. It was a really dark speech. The whole thing had one moment of light relief in it, one little joke, and that's what I missed.'

His horror, however, was to be short-lived. The next day, just as he was beating himself up with self-recrimination for fluffing his lines, the offers came flooding in. Among them was an approach from Jonathan Altaras from the London-based agency Jonathan Altaras Associates Limited. Altaras was struck by the young McGregor and was extremely keen to add his name to the company's already notable stable of actors. McGregor was astounded but quickly accepted.

The speed with which events subsequently unfolded was enough to render even him breathless. In his wildest dreams, he could never have envisaged being hijacked out of drama school a full six months early and pitchforked straight into the limelight in a lead role on national television. But that is exactly what happened.

'It's a funny thing,' McGregor later contemplated, 'when you want to become an actor you don't know quite where it's going to go. I wanted to get into drama school and put everything into getting there. And then you get there and you don't know what that's going to be like for three years. And then when you get out you don't know where you're gonna end up.'

Others, though, already believed that they had a very good idea of where he was headed and in his agent's opinion there was no time to lose in making a start. Not for McGregor the conventional path: being eased gradually out of drama school into the shallows of undemanding roles in provincial theatre, where any rough edges can be sympathetically smoothed. Instead he plunged in so far at the deep end that it was a case of getting his feet wet right up to his chest. And, characteristically, he revelled in it.

CHAPTER 3

Lipstick, Lust and Laughter

T HE PLUM ROLE that McGregor had landed was in *Lipstick On Your Collar*, a six-part musical romantic comedy series penned by the controversial and innovative British playwright Dennis Potter. By January 1992 pre-production work for Channel 4 was well advanced when, as producer Rosemarie Whitman recalls, they were contacted by McGregor's agent who had moved with lightning speed to try to put Ewan's name in the frame.

'He phoned our casting agent and said that he had newly signed a young actor and that we should see him. Well, it was very late in the day, so to speak, but we asked Ewan to come along on the Saturday morning which he did and he read opposite me and the director and we were both extremely impressed. Next I took him to our choreographer. She gave Ewan a piece of music and the steps and as soon as he started, she and I looked at each other and winked. He has a lovely singing voice and dances superbly. We didn't, however, want him to think that he had nothing more to do and so the choreographer put him fully through his paces.'

The character that McGregor was so successfully testing for was Private Mick Hopper, a young cockney doing his National Service as a Russian language clerk in the Military Intelligence Services of the British War Office in London. With just six weeks to go to demob he is bored out of his head at work and whiles away his time fantasising of a lustier love life and daydreaming of performing classic 1950s rock 'n' roll songs. It was a demanding role for someone not yet twenty-one. As Rosemarie Whitman says, 'Private Hopper was not a simple role to cast. He is a Jack the Lad –

but he's also more than that. There is another side to him and the actor who would portray him also had to be able to sing and dance. It was a difficult casting and we had screen-tested a lot of people, but when we saw Ewan, he was the only one we wanted. You take a chance, casting new blood.'

But Rosemarie Whitman's judgement proved to be sound when the six-month shoot for *Lipstick On Your Collar* began a few weeks later in March and carried on through the summer. This new musical was the final part of a trilogy that had started in 1978 with *Pennies From Heaven* and continued eight years later with the acclaimed *The Singing Detective*.

Dennis Potter's aim with *Lipstick On Your Collar* was to inject political overtones into a consummate blend of popular entertainment and social comment. Set in Fifties' Britain against the backdrop of the breaking Suez crisis, the story centres around the sweeping social and sexual revolution influenced by the explosion of American rock 'n' roll, with the main focus being on the thirst of the younger generation to establish its own identity. Pivotal to all this is Hopper and the vivid contrast between the dull, rigid formality of his working life and the intoxicating freedom that he finds in daydreaming of being a rock 'n' roll performer like Elvis Presley.

McGregor's portrayal of the fantasising, would-be rocker was solid, convincing and presented him with no great difficulty – even when handling the tricky lip-synch required to 'perform' the various numbers. Says Rosemarie Whitman, 'It was crucial to us that Ewan was up to this. Lip-synch is enormously difficult to do and if you don't get it exactly right, it blows the whole convention. We'd had to find a young actor who could sing well, dance well, lip-synch perfectly and also move like Elvis Presley.'

A tall order but the latter requirement, according to McGregor, came as almost second nature to him. 'When I was a kid I spent a lot of my time being Elvis Presley. There's something about his movies, the fact that they're so bad. But he was this cool guy who always had a good time and was always surrounded by beautiful women.'

McGregor even managed to look a little like the American legend, famous for throwing wicked glances from his sultry blue eyes and snarling his lip. He had been astonished to land the part in the first place but, quickly recovering, had dyed his hair black and thrown himself completely into character, pulsating pelvis, well-oiled swivel hips and all.

Says McGregor, 'Hopper imagines himself to be all the great rock 'n' rollers like Gene Vincent, Jerry Lee Lewis and Elvis Presley. And I got to be them all!'

Not all of the acts came so naturally though. 'I was really terrified when I did Gene Vincent,' he admitted, and was not helped much in this by the reaction of the extras hired for these particular sequences, a lot of whom had been rounded up from a Fifties' club and every one apparently a self-appointed expert. 'They kept shouting, "Nah, nah! That's not right!" ' recalls McGregor. 'It was bad enough having to do all this lip-synching for the cameras and act at the same time, never mind getting crits from every-one in the audience. It was good fun though.'

The producer puts it more strongly. 'He was great in the role,' she states. 'He was also wonderful to work with – so fascinated by and eager to learn from watching the other more experienced actors.'

Typical of many Dennis Potter dramas there was a fair bit of nudity. However, although McGregor would later acquire a reputation for 'get-ting his kit off' it did not start in this series. His only close encounter came with blonde cinema usherette Sylvia Berry (played by Louise Germaine): two bodies crushed against a wall, all dishevelled clothing and inelegant grunting. Says Rosemarie Whitman, 'We shot the series at Twickenham and Pinewood Film Studios as well as at various locations around London. It was a happy shoot with a young enthusiastic crew. Everyone was keen for it to do well.'

Including the playwright himself. Potter was renowned for taking a close interest in the working transformation of his writing from the page to the screen and he was present for the entire six months of filming. As in the case of parts one and two of the musical trilogy, much of *Lipstick On Your Collar* (Potter's last filmed television series), carried autobiograph-ical undertones. His life was dogged by illness and he would die a year after this final series was televised but he was a man who adored actors and liked being around them, and he certainly made a strong impact on McGregor.

'Ewan is a really courageous young man,' says Whitman. 'He was not at all put off with Dennis Potter being around – he was very courteous to Dennis.' In fact it went deeper than that as McGregor, soon after filming ended, recalled, 'I think he is a genius and although it took a while to get

ABOVE Ewan in his role as the obnoxious journalist Alex Law in the surprise hit movie *Shallow Grave*.

RIGHT Getting to grips with an increasingly psychotic flatmate David Stevens.

ABOVE Christopher Eccleston, Kerry Fox and Ewan shared the Hitchcock d'Argent Best Actor Award at the Dinard Film Festival for their performances in *Shallow Grave*.

With his French-born wife Eve Mavrakis, who Ewan met on set while filming the first episode of *Kavanagh QC* and later married in the Dordogne.

to know him, I really respect him. He's a brave man and had a lot of philosophical things to say about acting. He gave me a lot of very clued-up advice.'

Judging by the recollections of one of the older members of the cast this respect was reciprocal. Veteran stage and screen entertainer Roy Hudd played to perfection the seedy, sexually frustrated Harold Atterbow, the bespectacled cinema organist who lusts after usherette Sylvia. 'Sadly Ewan and I didn't have a scene together but I well remember watching some rushes with Dennis Potter and me saying to Potter, "You just can't take your eyes off that lad. When he's on the screen no one else is." Dennis replied, "Right. I do know how to pick 'em, don't I?" He certainly did.'

One person unlikely to be present then or at any point in the future when watching rushes is McGregor. He is characteristically blunt about it. 'I get bored with them. Some directors won't let you see them because they think you'll get paranoid but with me it's just boredom – tedious take after take of yourself.' His attitude to this early stage of production is at complete odds with his view of the final product. Whereas many actors modestly maintain that they are unable to look at themselves on screen, McGregor is not so self-effacing. 'I love it to death,' he has repeatedly stated. 'I love watching to see what I have done. It's fucking great.'

By the time filming for *Lipstick On Your Collar* ended in August 1992 McGregor had good reason to feel exuberant. Having run headlong into a starring role destined for television and one that required the kind of complex experience he could have been excused for not yet possessing, the experience had been a real baptism of fire. Yet, he had carried it off with immense professionalism. His naivety only showed afterwards when, as he has admitted, he sat about literally counting the days until the first episode was screened in the certain belief that from that moment on his professional life would instantly change for ever. But, at least in one sense, the heights to which he has since risen had little to do with *Lipstick On Your Collar*.

When Channel 4 screened the six-parter weekly commencing on 21 February 1993 it was not received as well as had been expected. According to Rosemarie Whitman most of the blame for this lies with the Press (Potter's most recent TV drama, *Blackeyes*, had been universally panned) and the problems her production company encountered in motivating their support. 'Ewan was clearly, even then, very talented. It was so obvious to myself and to the director and that was why we were so disappointed at not being able to attract Press attention for the series. They were just not interested in giving it promotion because it featured, as its main cast, four young actors. I so wanted *Lipstick On Your Collar* to actively *do* something for Ewan. We wanted it to be a bigger showcase for him, but it was a no-go with the Press.'

The whirlwind created by being plucked from drama school and catapulted straight into six months of demanding shooting had kept McGregor on a permanent high and in a hive of activity. Even so, he had managed along the way to fit in time to make his radio debut. Between 11 and 13 May 1992 he had joined the cast of a BBC World Service Play of the Week, *Tragic Prelude* by Alfonso Sastre, to rehearse and record under producer/director Hilary Norrish, with McGregor in one of the lead roles.

Set amidst the violence of Franco's dictatorship in Spain, this modern classic is a powerful study of terrorism and the effect it has both on its perpetrators and its victims. As Oscar, McGregor's task was to portray a bomber whose mission goes awry and who then is forced to cope with the resulting personal tragedy. According to co-star David Bannerman, radio debut or not, McGregor handled it like a pro.

'We all hit it off but out of the cast, John Hannah, myself and Ewan particularly came together and worked in really close harmony and, I think, as a result we got it so right. It was a nice play. Hilary Norrish was a great director and had cast it herself. From the start she knew the people she wanted for each role. Everyone had to know their character but she also made notes, gave them to us to study and then it was a case of getting on and doing it. Radio is very immediate. You have to be up to it instantly and Ewan was.'

McGregor recorded this in the middle of his work on *Lipstick On Your Collar* and quickly learned how to make the sudden jump from television acting to performing on radio. This can be bewildering even for a seasoned actor, as Bannerman points out. 'In radio everything about your character has to come through in the voice. It's not enough just to say the words. You have to project the character's whole personality, convey his thoughts and feelings about his actions. Every nuance has got to come alive for the listener and that's not easy. There's not much time for ironing things out either. For this kind of work you get together for a rehearsal, after which you talk over the part and discuss maybe which emphasis should go on which word and so on, but that is it. The read-through and the performance come very quickly together.' If McGregor suffered any crisis in confidence he knew where to look. Says Bannerman, 'Ewan knew I'd done a lot of radio and he would ask me plenty of questions, even down to which was the right side of the mike to use. He really was an extremely pleasant and very ordinary young man. The funny thing was, I'd been at drama school with Denis Lawson in Glasgow but at the time that we recorded this play I didn't know that this was Denis's nephew.'

The hour-long *Tragic Prelude* was transmitted on Sunday 7 June. A couple of months later McGregor returned to the BBC, this time to record a Radio Three play written by Tom Stoppard called *The Real Thing* which would be broadcast on 26 September 1993. But after that, suddenly, the whirlwind came to a halt. And, with no other work lined up, McGregor entered the vacuum of the ranks of the unemployed.

It is easy in such a precarious and densely populated profession for an actor to find himself adrift and rudderless. Actors can experience frequent, often lengthy, periods of 'resting', especially in the early stages of their career. The actors' union Equity has tens of thousands of members and, on average, about 80 per cent of those are out of work at any given time. In the autumn of 1992 McGregor too hit a fallow patch for a few weeks. During this time he drew unemployment benefit and scoured the job adverts in the weekly trade newspaper *The Stage*, prepared to consider any and all odds and ends on offer.

Although he was eagerly crossing off the days waiting for *Lipstick On Your Collar* to be screened, in all other respects McGregor had his feet firmly planted on the ground. He kept in close touch with his family back in Scotland and never wanted for friends, having forged strong bonds with fellow actors with whom he'd gone through drama school. And, despite his unemployed status, he enjoyed to the hilt his life in London, a city that he had quickly found he absolutely adored.

'There was a big gear change for me when I came to London. I'd go to parties at Denis Lawson's place, where I'd meet really great actors like

Zoe Wanamaker, Peter Capaldi and Richard E Grant, who I've since worked with.' Like most young actors he had had a taste of living in unsalubrious dives and being strapped for cash, but *Lipstick On Your Collar* had allowed all that to change. 'I remember when I'd moved into a beautiful flat near Denis, going up to Primrose Hill one night and looking down over London and feeling that I'd made it.'

Nevertheless, for someone so driven, who had seemingly bypassed the slower, lower-key introduction to acting and moved straight into the fast lane, it was intensely frustrating for McGregor to find himself suddenly stalled. Fortunately it wasn't a situation he was forced to endure for long. For, remarkably, this relatively brief period of professional inactivity turned out to be his one and only taste of unemployment and it ended when, in November 1992, he landed his first film role.

It was to be the smallest of bit parts, nothing to write home about, but in a cataclysmic year during which he had made both his television and radio debut, it was perhaps appropriate that he should make his film debut for good measure. The movie was *Being Human*, written and directed by Bill Forsyth, the Glasgow-born film-maker whose credits included the hit comedy *Gregory's Girl*. Forsyth had also been responsible for the 1983 movie *Local Hero* which had starred, among others, Denis Lawson and maybe it was this connection which led the writer to offer one of the small speaking parts in his latest project to Lawson's kin. His pitch to McGregor was certainly graphic; he is reported to have promised the footloose and fancy-free actor a spot of 'raping and pillaging as a hairy Highlander in Fort William'.

Such a colourful invitation was clearly too good to turn down and that month McGregor reported for duty in a film whose cast included the American actor Robin Williams as well as Britons Jonathan Hyde and Bill Nighy, with film producer David Puttnam, who had worked on *Local Hero*, once again teaming up with Forsyth at the helm. With a Warner Brothers' budget of $20 million it was an ambitious epic spanning five historical eras from the Bronze Age to modern-day America, the theme being man's eternal search for love and fulfilment. McGregor, who would spend a month on location in Morocco, entered the plot briefly as Alvarez, a shipwrecked sailor, and had only a single five-word line to deliver; 'I'll do it, Don Parlo.' But, as the cliche goes, it was not so much what he said, as the way in which he said it. Seasoned producer David Puttnam was ahead of the game in noticing his latent potential.

'Ewan is a terrific actor. He is very fortunate in that from early on the camera clearly loved him. On *Being Human* it became immediately obvious, and not just to me. I vividly recall the scene where he was standing in a group of people and yet he was so prominent, to the point that I spoke to the cameraman and the production assistants about it. We decided then that we ought to build up his part, specifically create more scenes for him, which we did and shot them. When it came to the edit, however, these extra scenes were lacerated.' Lord Puttnam goes on, 'McGregor has the same quality that a certain select group of actors have. Once you watch them they mesmerise you and you forget that you are watching an actor because they appeal to you personally.'

One of the production assistants with whom David Puttnam consulted was Natasha Ross. She insists it was clear even then that McGregor was destined for greater things; as someone who tipped both Ralph Fiennes and Jude Law for future stardom, she is clearly a sound judge of talent. 'Ewan was under-used in the film. He was very good, which doesn't often become that apparent in such a tiny part as he had. What was most noticeable about him was his general confidence. He had very good discipline on set which, again, was surprising in such a young actor not long out of drama school. He had a distinct air of assurance and took any direction in his stride. He certainly did not suffer from nerves.'

Despite the fact that the extra scenes he shot had failed to make it into the final cut, the level of recognition which had prompted David Puttnam and the others to try to flesh out his bit part must have helped bolster McGregor's already sturdy belief in himself. This was his first taste of film work, so very different to either television or radio, and he now knew where his future ultimately lay. Natasha Ross concurs, 'He was certainly ambitious and completely in love with film. Off-set he was very much a young enthusiastic lad, yet we all got the distinct impression that he would much rather talk of movies and movie-making than charge off down the beach.'

Whilst it was true that McGregor's passion for acting was all-encompassing, he also knew how to party. Co-star Jonathan Hyde recalls,

'It might have been a big-budget Warner Brothers movie, but I must say a lot of the exterior facilities were exceptionally drab and the trailers were unspeakable.' The solution was simple. As Hyde puts it, 'We'd pass our spare time visiting fairs and some just went and got drunk in Marrakesh. All of us had many a late boozy night and as for Ewan – he sings like the devil and will play the guitar at the drop of a hat. We had a lot of good laughs.'

The good time had making the movie unfortunately was not mirrored by success when it was released. *Being Human* ended up being left on the shelf for a year and when it was finally released, in America, it was a box-office flop. Warner Brothers were again to be disappointed when it was screened at the 1994 Edinburgh Film Festival. In the circumstances it had been decided that reaction to this showing would determine whether the Festival screening of *Being Human* would end up constituting its one and only UK cinema outing. Reviews proved to be mixed but descriptions such as 'still-born' and 'ill-conceived' dominated and so ensured the final ignominy of it being sent direct to video in Britain.

When McGregor left Morocco to return to winter in Britain he was unaware of the film's sad fate. But one thing was for sure: he himself was far from being redundant. He was due to commence six weeks' of theatre rehearsals immediately on his return. He had been cast as Nicholas Beckett, the over-sexed hotel pageboy in the classic adult comedy *What The Butler Saw* by Joe Orton.

Orton's last play, infused by the real-life drama of his violent death at the hands of his lover Kenneth Halliwell, is often considered to be his finest work. It had received its London debut on 5 March 1969 at the Queen's Theatre with Ralph Richardson in the leading role and was famously booed from the gallery. Hailed since as one of the most perfectly constructed comedy classics in English literature, this 'bedroom' farce is a satirised celebration of neurosis. The production in which McGregor had secured a part was to be performed at the Playhouse in the cathedral town of Salisbury; directed by Penny Ciniewicz, it was scheduled to launch the theatre's new season on 21 January 1993. Six characters form the nucleus of the two-act play and so McGregor joined National Theatre actor Jeremy Child, star of numerous television dramas Isla Blair,

Roger Sloman, Paul Viragh and Jacqueline Defferary, who like McGregor would be chalking up her first professional stage job since leaving drama school.

In his short lifetime Joe Orton had held a deep loathing for psychiatrists and this madhouse farce, dubbed 'sublimely filthy' by the *Sunday Times*, is proof of that. It is set in a psychiatric clinic and practically everyone at some point loses the thread of events, their wits and, especially, part or all of their clothes. Attempting to summarise the fast-paced lunacy Isla Blair collapsed it to, 'A shocking play about nymphomania, homosexuality and transvestism, all treated as if they were mental illness.'

As the resourceful bell-hop McGregor attacked the role with his usual boundless enthusiasm, starting from the moment when he arrived for rehearsals alongside accomplished actress Isla Blair. Curvaceous and vivacious, she had carved out a reputation for playing sexually liberated women; she became notorious when, at the age of forty-eight, she defied the dictum that actresses should after a certain age withdraw gracefully into character roles and instead engaged in nude love scenes in 'The Final Cut', the third part of the popular BBC 1 drama series *House Of Cards*. This play was to be her first steady engagement at Salisbury Playhouse and she recalls, 'I first met Ewan the day after New Year's Day and it was deep snow. We all met for a read-through and it went fine. Straightaway I found him extremely courteous, warm and nice to everybody. He was never standoffish – very much part of the team.'

As usual McGregor was keen to glean whatever he could from the rest of the cast and in Isla Blair's case she had performed this play before. Almost fourteen years earlier at the Old Vic in London she had taken the role of the innocent young secretary, here handled by Defferary; this time around she had the role of the nymphomaniac wife of mad psychoanalyst Dr Prentice (played by Jeremy Child).

This version of the Sixties farce, however, was to be different. Award-winning director Penny Ciniewicz had chosen to update it to the 1990s – a ploy which turned out, in many people's eyes, to be less than successful. It was felt by some experienced watchers that the play became a kind of customised version of what Orton had really intended and ran shy of delving deep into the playwright's more disturbingly contentious perceptions. One casualty of Ciniewicz's approach was McGregor's character.

Nicholas Beckett became a faded version of himself, less menacing and manipulative a presence than in Orton's original. Although the farce played to packed houses, Isla Blair agrees with much of the criticism.

'To be honest the production was not very good. It is a Sixties play and to work it really has to stay that way. Trying to update it rendered it very odd. It came from a strange angle and was sexist and politically incorrect for the Nineties. A lot of the time the audience were left a bit embarrassed.' She goes on, 'Having said that, there were some very funny moments. There is a scene when Ewan has to run across the stage completely naked and then cover himself up with a policeman's helmet. I am stripped down to stockings and a flimsy black lacy petticoat and when you're doing this kind of thing night after night, waiting together in the wings like this, then you get to know each other quite well!'

The play's preoccupation with nudity in fact moved one critic to commiserate with McGregor, 'It can't be easy making your stage debut without clothes,' he said. But his sympathy was misplaced: McGregor has an unabashed and uninhibited enjoyment of stripping off in public. Years later, likening himself to his hero, comedian Billy Connolly, he declared, 'He likes getting his kit off and so do I!' Reflecting on the number of occasions he would undress for roles he also revealed, 'I've been naked in loads of things. I fucking love it. I especially enjoyed being nude in the play *What The Butler Saw* for the tweedy fraternity in Salisbury. People were dying in the aisles. Old ladies were having coronaries.'

Actors generally define stage work as getting back to their roots. For McGregor, having worked in the twelve months since leaving drama school in television, radio and film, it provided him with valuable experience of the fourth medium of his craft. However, whilst *What the Butler Saw* was his professional stage debut, it would prove to be at least five years before he would return to the boards. But his five-week run in Orton's farce garnered him important lessons in expressiveness, if nothing else. Says Isla Blair, 'As far as craft goes, on film and television you often don't have to actually act. It's enough to concentrate hard on what you are thinking about and the camera will pick it up. On stage, however, your reactions must be heightened and you need a presence. Some actors are great on screen and don't have the same effect on stage and vice versa.' In summing up McGregor's handling of Nicholas Beckett she continues,

'Ewan was fine, not at all bad – but it wasn't his finest hour. Having said that it wasn't any of our finest hours.'

That said, the two actors formed a friendship offstage. 'Ewan has great charm,' states Blair. 'I used to give him a lift back to London at weekends. Sometimes it was just the two of us . . . if we were alone he began to be able to tell me little personal things, secrets. He was able to unburden himself at least a little. But mostly we had a good laugh. Both of us adore Billy Connolly's humour and mostly we played his tapes and spent the entire journey to London in stitches.'

Socially they also would spend time together during the week in Salisbury. McGregor's close friend, actor Jude Law who he had met at drama school, would come down to support McGregor in the play and afterwards a group of the cast and their friends would go out on the town. Isla Blair is married to Shakespearean actor Julian Glover and together they have a son, Jamie, who is also an actor. She says, 'Jamie came to see the play and with Ewan, Jude and some others we went out to dinner. Jude is exactly like Ewan – there is nothing snotty or grand about him. They're both extremely nice and remarkably down-to-earth young men.'

Although Isla's opinion of McGregor's stage performance was ambivalent, she wholeheartedly joined the growing chorus of approval regarding his long-term prospects. 'By the time the play's run was coming to an end he was preparing for his next role back in television and I said to Jamie, "You know, there's something about Ewan. There is no question that he is going to be a star." Sometimes you don't need to be a great actor to have star quality. In Ewan, though, there was definitely an indefinable something and it's not just because he's got this slightly naughty, cheeky quality and a twinkle in his eyes. He has a tenderness about him too. Behind the toughs and the cynical guys he went on to portray in *Shallow Grave* and *Trainspotting* there is a vulnerability about him that's very engaging. He's like this in real life as well as projecting it on screen.'

McGregor's stint at the Salisbury Playhouse came to an end on 13 February 1993. Preparations for his next role were already well underway. He was to take the romantic lead in a BBC production of Stendhal's *Scarlet And Black*, taking on the mantle of a French schemer and adventurer. Of

McGregor's performance as Nicholas Beckett, Peter Blacklock, a theatre critic with the *Salisbury Journal*, had shrewdly concluded, 'Let's keep an eye on Ewan. We could have seen the birth of a fine career.' Perhaps, McGregor must have thought, his return to the small screen in such a high-profile part would confirm this? It was certainly considered in 1993 television casting circles that he had landed 'the role of the year'.

CHAPTER 4

Gallic Charmer

THE ROLE OF Julien Sorel in *Scarlet And Black* was the first lead role that McGregor desperately wanted to secure. Sorel is an ambitious French peasant who, using his looks, wits and talent to manipulate, seduces his way up through the higher echelons of society via the army and the church. *Le Rouge Et Le Noir* was the second novel and first masterpiece of the nineteenth-century writer Henri Marie Beyle, better known by his pseudonym, Stendhal. It is a story of passion, ambition and intrigue. It had been adapted by Stephen Lowe as a sumptuous new £4 million costume drama, to be produced by Rosalind Wolfes (now Anderson) and directed by Ben Bolt, son of the Oscar-winning English dramatist Robert Bolt. A lot of hopes were riding on it.

The three-part period production boasted a cast comprising a mix of familiar and fresh faces, among them T P McKenna, Joseph O'Conor, Stratford Johns, Martin Jarvis, Alice Krige and newcomer Rachel Weisz. The six-week initial shoot was due to begin after Easter in April 1993, taking McGregor off to the Franche-Comté region of south-eastern France, on location in the jagged Jura mountains, to the Old Quarter in Lyon, Dijon and Dole as well as the cathedral in Besancon and various chateaux.

As soon as McGregor learned he had a chance to play the tragic hero Sorel he was immediately fired up to get the part – not surprisingly since it was considered to be a major showcase television role for a young actor. *Lipstick On Your Collar* had ended its six-week run on Channel 4 to a muted reception which, for McGregor, had proved to be something of a disappointment. 'I was convinced I would wake up the morning after it was shown and everything would be different. Of course, it wasn't.' Resilience, however, resided in every notch of his spine and it had made him even more determined to win this sought-after BBC TV role.

The importance of casting wisely when it came to the charismatic and scheming Julien Sorel was not lost on the director. 'The first thing that struck me on reading the book was that if we couldn't get the right Julien, it wasn't worth making the film at all.'

They were looking for a young, good-looking actor who could convey an intriguing blend of innocence and insidious sex appeal; moreover, that someone had to be capable of displaying an inner passion tempered by outward self-control. In many ways the real-life McGregor fitted the role like a glove. His inherent natural spirit coupled to an indefatigable enthusiasm produces an explosive combination of excess within control, fuelling the vibrancy with which he attacks his whole life. But if he had made up his mind that he was perfect for this part, it did not seem to him that, initially, Bolt agreed.

McGregor has since revealed, 'I am very ambitious. I always wanted to be an actor and took no notice of people who tried to put me off. It was the same with getting this part. The first time I went to see Ben, I got the impression that I wasn't what he was looking for. The second time, I was determined to make him change his mind.'

In fact, his perception that he had a battle on his hands to get the role was wrong, as producer Ros Anderson recalls. 'We searched far and wide for the right Julien Sorel and we had seen quite a few actors before Ewan bowled through the door and took both Ben Bolt and myself completely by surprise. Bowled over indeed is the appropriate description. I know he insists that he was nervous at his first interview and felt that because of that he hadn't done well, but he had. His is an interesting generation of actors but in Ewan we found that something extra that was needed, because the character of Julien Sorel required so many different things. He is born a peasant but aspires to be a gentleman. With Ewan I saw that earthiness and I knew that equally he could convey the stature required to carry off the pretence of being a gentleman.'

McGregor was easily able to relate his own sense of ambition to that of the character's. He describes Sorel as someone 'extraordinarily proud, angry, arrogant and brave. He is driven by this obsessive desire to succeed, yet he never purposefully does anyone any harm.'

This was also to be a bed-hopping role and McGregor was a young man already acutely sensitised to the sensuality of acting, from the days when he had responded to the physical allure of pantomime actresses dressed in fishnet stockings. Now, a year after having bumped and ground his way through *Lipstick On Your Collar* as a twentieth-century rock 'n' roller, he faced the prospect of portraying a dashing seducer of the mid-1800s. Typically, he had distinct views about what this would mean for him. 'It was such a sexy time,' he maintained during filming, 'a lot sexier than the 1950s. I get to wear very tight trousers and short jackets with tails, so it'll be all hips again.'

Scarlet And Black is a story heaving with agony and ecstasy, self-advancement and self-denial, as well as illicit sex and passionate revenge, culminating in what is hailed as one of classic literature's most famously shocking and dramatic conclusions when Julien Sorel, having murdered his married mistress, is imprisoned, tried and eventually guillotined. It is the kind of gutsy red-blooded role in a lavish and romantic production that would appeal to most young actors and, as Ros Anderson recalls, McGregor eagerly handled every facet of it.

'It was a learning process for him,' she says, 'and it was a big thing to land on his shoulders when he did not have a lot of experience, but he showed great spirit. He's very intelligent but what came over strongly was how he brought so much energy to the part. One of the main themes is this young man sexually attracted to an older woman and he brought that earthy quality that I noticed at casting which effortlessly created the necessary understanding as to how this good and pure wife, who had never thought of straying, could be seduced by this passionate and intense young man. For her it is a voyage of discovery. For him it is social climbing. He is very ambitious, tenacious, and Ewan was perfectly able to project that vaunting ambition, yet at the same time he managed to let the viewer see glimpses of another, more vulnerable side, just enough so that he managed not to come across as heartless, soulless and ruthless.'

In contrast to the many social and sexual tensions on set, the prevailing sense during filming was of how much fun McGregor was to work with. Says Anderson, 'He was always laughing which was even more suprising since he didn't much like the restraint of the costumes and there was a lot of heavy stuff in the role but he was a delight to work with.' McGregor, his hair once again dyed black for the part, certainly had a ball doing it. 'It was all terribly exciting,' he glows with enthusiasm. 'The riding, the sword-fighting, the action. There was a real kick in it.'

On at least one occasion the 'kick' was a shade too literal when the charger he was sitting on unexpectedly threw him, and McGregor ended up dangerously beneath half a ton of plunging, panicking horse. 'I was part of a guard of honour waiting to greet the King. My horse was meant to rear up with the excitement of it all but the first time it went up, I came flying off. Then I must have squeezed him in the wrong way so he went even farther up. I came off sideways and didn't let go of the reins, which pulled him down on top of me.' Potentially the accident was lethal, but McGregor escaped with only a slightly sprained knee and for this he credits the animal. 'If the horse had been less experienced I would have had a broken leg but I am quite sure he deliberately came down very gently. I swear to God he was trying not to hurt me.'

The producer recalls this hair-raising incident very clearly. 'He had put in a great deal of training for his riding and he had some difficult and demanding things to do. The horseback sequences in *Scarlet And Black* were challenging for the horsemen and for the actors, and Ewan had to do both. It was a great disappointment to him when he fell off his horse, particularly because he had prepared hard for that scene. He loves taking on a challenge, though, and wanted to immediately do it again but I stepped in and said no. There was a massive amount of action with horsemen charging in all directions, carriages thundering around and cannons blasting away and it was then that his horse had thrown him. He was so crestfallen that I wouldn't let him do it again but it was my job to protect him as the star of the drama. One of the stunt co-ordinators kept saying how Kevin Costner did all his own stunts in *Robin Hood Prince Of Thieves* but I said, "Ewan's my baby and I'm not having him hurt." '

Setting aside his frustration, when the production broke for a timely lunch McGregor simply strapped a packet of frozen vegetables to his knee to stop it swelling then carried on filming in the afternoon. Undeterred by this early mishap, when a stunt double was not employed he was more than keen to handle most of the other action scenes himself.

Similarly, he required no stunt double when it came to action of a more tender kind in the bedroom. Performing love scenes can cause anxieties for actors of all ages. Hollywood star Michael Douglas has remarked on how stressful they can be, representing as they do one of the rare areas in screen acting where nearly everyone can be a judge. And Michael Caine has revealed his preference to avoid them altogether; it proves to be too much like hard work trying to convince the wife later that he did not enjoy it. And nerves can just as easily afflict the younger generation of actors, as McGregor's contemporary, Chris O'Donnell, co-star along with George Clooney in one of the *Batman* movies has testified. 'They're weird to do and even weirder to watch.' He recalled the moment when with friends he visited a cinema to watch *Mad Love*, in which he had a sex scene with Drew Barrymore; he had to sneak out of the darkened theatre when the bedroom scene came on, because he was too embarrassed to see himself on celluloid.

The contrast between O'Donnell and McGregor could hardly be sharper. Doubtless bolstered by his total lack of inhibition about nudity, every time Julien Sorel is incited to bed a lady by Napoleon's war cry 'To arms!', McGregor responded with alacrity. 'Simulating what is really a private act in front of millions of people isn't really an issue. It's just like doing dance steps. I wasn't uptight about it because Alice and Rachel weren't. They just went with the scene. They were brilliant.'

Ros Anderson remembers, 'There was one day of shooting when he was naked almost the entire day. There is a scene in which he has to escape from Madame de Renal's [his mistress's] bedroom. He climbs down a ladder naked and gets to the ground, only to be immediately chased for his life by Monsieur de Renal blasting off a shotgun. As he makes a run for it we did the bare botty shot with him, I think, clutching some crumpled clothes to his front. But once we did that scene, we had to do all sorts of other pick-up shots in different locations and he spent all the time in – mostly out – of dressing gowns and he made it all such a laugh, injecting a kind of naughtiness, as if it were streaking.' She adds, 'He wasn't so comfortable when we had to get him to pose with Alice and Rachel for photographs, not with them undressed but in a state of disarray. Posing was clearly different for him to the process of acting a part.'

Directors look for the truthfulness of an actor's performance and this McGregor delivered in spades – as two of his co-stars testify. The versatile actor/director Joseph O'Conor played the part of Father Chelan, the elderly parish priest in Julian Sorel's home town. O'Conor has this to say of McGregor, 'He is wonderfully sensitive to work with and picks everything up very quickly. It was my job to teach him Latin. I was his mentor and he had a great deal to say in Latin. I taped it for Ewan to learn and it was difficult stuff, some of which, I may say, he had to carry off with an air of scorn and contempt, which is mighty hard. Yet he picked it up perfectly and never once got so much as a syllable wrong.'

He goes on. 'Julien Sorel is one of the greatest parts in literature. It's often compared to Hamlet. In the end he makes no effort to save himself from execution. Throughout Ewan gave a quite astonishing performance. For me he showed an extraordinary ease. He has that light in his head that really great actors have. It goes with an assumption, with no conceit, that he is going upwards. There is no side to him, though. He is very democratic, professionally.'

His on-screen ability to communicate brings praise too from television stalwart Stratford Johns, who appeared as the florid-faced Abbe Pirard, the stern but compassionate master of the seminary to which young Sorel is sent. Says Stratford Johns, 'We had several scenes together and he was extremely good in the part. Although this was a big role for Ewan to land without a lot of experience at that stage he never once gave cause for any of us to give it a thought. In all our scenes he reacted beautifully to me, and I to him. He was a very professional and charming young man.'

McGregor was as popular with the crew as with the cast, all of whom had worked hard in the midst of the picturesque villages and verdant French countryside to bring the complex, passionate and very Gallic tale alive. The BBC is renowned for its consummate skill in producing costume dramas and *Scarlet And Black* certainly dripped with style – but in one sense the production had been up against it from the start.

In 1954 there had been a French/Italian film of *Le Rouge Et Le Noir* by director Claude Autant-Lara, at three hours long it had ultimately been classified as a massive attempt to conquer an unfilmable novel. What the

#5
RENTON

Trainspotting

DUE TO ARRIVE:
23:02:96
From the makers of
Shallow Grave

The face that launched a thousand trips…

ABOVE So anxious was *Trainspotting* actress Kelly Macdonald about filming this explicit sex scene that she spent most of the time leading up to the shoot in the toilet.

RIGHT Mark Renton preparing to shoot up – one of the many shocking scenes that made *Trainspotting* so controversial.

BELOW As Renton, Ewan showed the unglamorous lows of heroin addiction as well as the highs.

BBC had put together now was three seventy-five-minute episodes and Joseph O'Conor, for one, felt this was insufficient. 'It was a very good script but the book needed at least six episodes. As a result, [the production] was too crowded and I didn't think it came off. It is a terribly difficult novel to do visually. It's packed with philosophy and there are certainly no descriptions of bonking at all – they were inserted in this version. So although the script was well done, they had not been given enough time in which to really do it justice.'

When filming finished in France there were several more weeks of filming in Britain, ending mid-summer. Learning from past experience, McGregor refused to fall into the same trap as he had after completing *Lipstick On Your Collar*. 'I should have put it behind me and just got on with life. So after *Scarlet And Black* I walked away and did something else. Mind you, it wasn't easy. The whole job was all-consuming from start to finish. I've never felt as passionate about anything as I have about this.'

He did not have so long to wait this time between the end of filming and seeing the finished product on screen. *Scarlet And Black* transmitted in a prime-time Sunday night slot at 9.05 pm – just past the watershed – on BBC 1 between 31 October and 14 November 1993. The critics were less than enthusiastic. Some reviewers criticised McGregor's Julien Sorel as 'irredeemably modern' – missing the point that the producers had wanted an updated feel to *Scarlet And Black*. One critic also felt that he lacked sufficient weight in the role. 'He's meant to be a young man in the grip of a demonic form of ambition,' he wrote, 'and yet he struts around looking like a young David Essex.'

In terms of ratings though, the viewing figures for the drama almost matched that of another BBC period piece, the highly acclaimed *Middlemarch*. What stood out, apart from the expected praise of its visual delights, were the plaudits from certain critics for McGregor's performance. There was much talk of his 'compelling gaze'. Those reviewers who had already predicted fame for the young Scot found themselves to be vindicated with this new serial. One *Daily Express* journalist declared that, if nothing else, the lavish *Scarlet And Black* would 'surely make a star of Ewan McGregor, the striking twenty-two-year old actor.'

In one sense McGregor was entitled to lap up these compliments. He was 'the new kid on the block', in a mere eighteen months he had played the lead in two high-profile TV dramas and made a respectable debut in the demanding world of radio; in addition he had made his stage and film debuts and, along the way, earned the respect and affection of screenwriters, directors, producers and actors alike.

Yet, on the flip side of the coin, both television dramas had been viewed critically as falling below par; the one film in which he had appeared had flopped; and his stage work, according to a co-star, had not been his finest hour. He was rapidly gaining in experience and was just as determined as ever to shine but the springboard to success he yearned for had thus far eluded him. When he was sent to audition for a part in a low budget grant-assisted Scottish film made by an untried and untested team comprising a first-time writer, producer and director, it's perhaps unsurprising that, at first, no one realised McGregor was about to make his breakthrough.

The origins of the film *Shallow Grave* go back to more than a year before its makers made their first appeal for finance in July 1992. John Hodge, a junior doctor at the Eastern General Hospital in Edinburgh, had spent his off-duty rest periods in the early mornings between shifts pursuing his creative ambitions, writing a screenplay about a group of flatmates whose lives are changed (and the seamier side of their personalities unpicked) by an unexpected and traumatic event concerning the apartment's newest tenant.

Hodge reveals how he conceived the idea. 'I thought there was a good story in sharing a flat, but I didn't think the friction of friendship was enough in itself. I thought it needed an extreme dramatic twist. That's when I came up with the idea of the body and the money and all that stuff. For me it really just reflects the normal arguments that people have, only on a grander, more extreme scale.'

For a long time the project had been no more than the private passion of a single individual. Then Hodge showed part of his early work to another Scot, Andrew Macdonald, whom he met at the 1991 Edinburgh Film Festival. Macdonald turned out to be the grandson of Emeric Pressburger, one half of The Archers film-making partnership with the legendary Michael Powell; Powell and Pressburger were responsible for some of the most memorably innovative British films of the 1940s and 1950s. Hodge was most impressed. At the time Macdonald was working as a locations manager for the gritty STV detective drama series *Taggart*, but he harboured strong ambitions to become a film producer. From that point on he and Hodge trod a dogged path together, to realise their joint dream of making a feature film.

Macdonald states, 'We began in the belief that the script had to be perfect before we even thought about financiers. From the start we were looking at our market and also writing for a film that would not cost more than £1 million. It was for a *Blood Simple* or *Reservoir Dogs* audience and I became a complete addict of facts on how independent American films were made, down to the tiniest detail of budgets and shooting schedules, before we approached people.'

That first approach had been to The Scottish Film Production Fund, whose Chairman, Allan Scott, decided that it was the best script he had read in years. As a result they were offered an initial sum of £4000 (later increased), which enabled John Hodge to develop his treatment. Then in August 1992, at the Edinburgh Film Festival, Andrew Macdonald made significant ground when a spoof video he had made on how to find film funding, in which such cinematic heavyweights as director Michael Winner and former James Bond star Sean Connery had appeared, was screened. The upshot was that Macdonald was introduced to the three main backers of British films – British Screen, and the television companies BBC and Channel 4.

Of these three corporations, Macdonald knew that the latter shelled out almost three-quarters of a million pounds to about a dozen films per year. He lost no time in hotfooting it soon after to the Highlands and the annual film-makers' conference in Inverness. His quarry there was David Aukin, head of Channel 4 Films; Macdonald was determined that Aukin should at least read Hodge's script. He succeeded in getting the influential film executive to take the script away with him.

Just a few weeks later Aukin was on the telephone to Macdonald arranging a meeting at the Channel 4 offices in London in early December. It was not only the project which appealed to David Aukin; the depth of Macdonald's preparation impressed him too. He says of *Shallow Grave*, 'I liked this from the start because it had a great script and they knew what they were doing.' He adds a note of caution. 'But you never know which ones are going to be a hit.'

With the ball beginning to roll Channel 4 Films originally budgeted their contribution to be around £800,000; this was subsequently topped up with another £50,000 and in the end the final budget rested at £1,043,000. That figure included monies from other sources, in particular a grant of £150,000 obtained from the newly established Glasgow Film Fund. *Shallow Grave* was to be the first feature film project to benefit from this Fund – the grant represented its entire first-year budget. This award was viewed by some as rather rash, but it was felt that *Shallow Grave* had the potential to do well and could put Glasgow on the film-making map. The film's producer was certainly in no doubt as to its importance. Andrew Macdonald told reporters, 'This is fantastic news. We already had £850,000 funding from Channel 4, but we needed the Glasgow Film Fund to fill the funding gap. The project could not have gone ahead without the GFF.'

With the finance in place, the script underwent a series of rewrites. 'The first draft was incredibly long-winded and ponderous,' admitted John Hodge. 'In fact, I found it easier learning to become a doctor, than a scriptwriter.' And by now a director had been welcomed on board. He was Danny Boyle, the Lancashire-born former artistic director of London's Royal Court Theatre, who had directed a couple of television series, including most recently the acclaimed BBC serial based on Jane Roger's book *Mr Wroe's Virgins*. *Shallow Grave* would be his debut in feature film direction and, like Macdonald, he was extremely excited about the script.

He reveals why: 'Unlike most British writing for the screen, it was simple, very dynamic and didn't carry a lot of history or moral baggage with it. Its milieu was very British but its total concentration on the storyline seemed to me like the best of American cinema.'

This transatlantic influence was no coincidence, as John Hodge declares, 'When I began, I'd seen a succession of American films which had one thing in common – a small group of people working out their differences in a tight situation over a short period of time. With the script of *Shallow Grave* it was important that something happened every page or so. Character has to be grafted onto a healthy narrative so with this film there's not too much heart-searching. It is better to be a little glib than to be over-portentous.'

Producer Andrew Macdonald believed that *Shallow Grave's* style of story-telling was reminiscent of a combination of US independent movie forerunners, with the craft of old Hollywood thrown in. 'This is hopefully a young, hip, funny, contemporary Scottish thriller – slightly raw, slightly shocking, which will probably make people laugh in some odd places.' Shooting for what this animated and unified trio were modestly pitching as 'a good B-movie' was due to commence in September 1993, with plans for it to be completed in time for entry to the following year's Cannes Film Festival. During that summer, when McGregor had completed *Scarlet And Black*, they were about to begin casting.

Although the BBC's new costume drama had yet to be transmitted, television executives and casting directors were already prepared to stick their necks out and publicly promote Ewan McGregor. At that time, casting for the male lead in a forthcoming film adaptation of the latest bestselling Jilly Cooper novel had attracted an unusual level of Press speculation and when asked by one national newspaper to put forward their personal suggestions both Mary Selway and Alan Ayres opted for McGregor. Selway, a leading casting director for films such as *Hope And Glory* and *Aliens*, believed him ideal because, 'He's very mischievous,' whilst Ayres, a BBC spokesman for drama, went further. 'McGregor is the rising star this autumn. He's very heart-throbbing.'

But McGregor's eyes were not turned on another romance, nor did he at this juncture particularly wish to play another Englishman. In terms of accent he possesses one of Scotland's more attractive lilts and, having portrayed an English wide-boy, a Spanish terrorist and a French peasant-turned-gentleman he had yet to use his native tongue. He was busy telling reporters, 'I am desperate to do something in my own accent.' Playing the character Alex Law in *Shallow Grave* would just fit the bill and his agent secured him an audition. 'It was just a normal casting,' says McGregor. 'I was just sent along to meet them.'

He landed the part without knowing that he had been partly helped to it by his friend, producer Ros Anderson. She says, 'Just after shooting ended on *Scarlet And Black* I got a telephone call from Danny Boyle. I'd worked with Danny on *Mr Wroe's Virgins* and he asked if I could send him tapes of Ewan. Well, we didn't have tapes available just then, but anyway I told him, "You *should* see Ewan McGregor – you will love him. He is incredibly versatile." '

The ninety-two-minute *Shallow Grave* reflected the democratic attitude between writer, producer and director in that it was to feature, not one central lead, but three; a female doctor, Juliet Miller, for which the New Zealand actress Kerry Fox, the star of the Jane Campion-directed film *An Angel At My Table*, would be cast, and two young men – David Stevens, a chartered accountant handled by Christopher Eccleston, and McGregor's character, Alex Law, a tabloid journalist. These three yuppies occupy a spacious upmarket apartment in Scotland's capital. The story begins as they interview a string of prospective candidates for a fourth flatmate to help meet the rent. After callously, sometimes cruelly, dismissing many applicants they choose a man they believe to be a high-flying businessman, Hugo, played by Keith Allen.

Matters quickly unravel when, the day after moving in, Hugo is found dead on his bed and a suitcase tantalisingly containing £2 million in used banknotes is discovered in his room. The combination of the stranger's dangerous drug-dealing associates who come looking for their money, and the three yuppies' decision to dismember and dispose of the body and keep the cash, only to plot individually to cheat each other, provides the basis for an energetic, fast-paced black comedy/thriller which openly savages the divisive greed of Margaret Thatcher's Britain. It is both funny, in a mordant sense, and sickeningly violent.

The film's originality would play a strong part in its success. From the outset the audience is intentionally made to feel a total lack of empathy for the three main players in the story, each one superior, self-centred and conceited to a fault. The lack of at least one 'good' character to warm to bravely ran the risk of completely alienating the audience and rendering it coldly indifferent to the fate of the protagonists. But, strangely, the initial repulsion segues into an involuntary compulsion to follow the plot; so hooked upon these nasty individuals does the viewer become that, when the police show up asking questions about the dead drug-dealer, there is a palpable but unfathomable sense of hope that the unlikeable trio will escape detection. A truly modern morality tale.

The open nastiness and materialistic cynicism of Alex Law, coming hard on the heels of Julien Sorel's concealed calculation and contempt, enabled McGregor to explore ways of portraying essentially similar traits in different ways. His was a consummate performance. He infused the long-haired, obnoxiously smug journalist with the ability to attract whilst being offensive or even irritating. Although he displays a momentary vulnerability when, as a reporter, he is sent to cover the breaking story of a body found clumsily buried in a shallow grave, at all other times he projects an unerring shrewdness. It is no surprise that, when the final double-cross comes, although Alex in the climatic explosion of gratuitous violence is left looking like a victim with a serious stab wound, he has in fact manipulated matters so that, with David dead, Juliet is caught for his own attempted murder. Meanwhile, Alex is left lying literally a plank's width away from the stash of money he had earlier hidden under the now blood-soaked floor boards.

On a lighter note McGregor also displayed beautifully the natural ability to extract comedy from often grim and vicious dialogue. Such as when, along with his flatmates, he attends a charity benefit night in aid of sick children. Immediately stung on discovering this, he loudly objects to Juliet. 'I *hate* children,' Alex says. 'I'd raise money to have the little fuckers put down!' McGregor once hinted that he had sometimes struggled to be at ease portraying such an objectionable and aggressive person but ultimately it was a role which did not particularly stretch him. 'I really like playing such a cocky character, but sometimes I don't find it very challenging.'

For McGregor, the making of this first major feature film provided an added pleasure; it took him back to Scotland on a professional basis for the first time. Shooting spread over September into October 1993; although the film was set in Edinburgh filming actually took place mainly in and around Glasgow, in particular in a large empty warehouse which had been turned into a studio at Anniesland. Here, an entire Edinburgh Georgian flat had been recreated at a cost which knocked a hole in the movie's limited budget. McGregor's raid back across the border gave some of his hometown mates the chance to catch up with their rapidly rising friend; he delighted in taking time out to go drinking with them at a Stockbridge pub after their arranged visit to the set was over. And his mother Carol got in on the act when, having turned up on the set one day, she was roped into playing one of the unsuccessful flatshare applicants. She survived the edit to appear in the film in the briefest blink of an eye.

But the source of McGregor's biggest joy was the experience of working with the three-man team behind the film, all of whom were in their thirties and had a refreshingly unique outlook on the whole process of movie-making. For the Boyle, Macdonald and Hodge partnership *Shallow Grave* would form a highly successful debut into the world of cinema, just as this film would prove to be McGregor's acknowledged breakthrough role. It is understandable that the experience should have heralded the beginning of a deep and lasting bond of respect and friendship between the four.

Screenwriter John Hodge partly revealed the explanation for the threesome's working harmony when he remarked, 'Working with a producer and a director who were also making their first feature film meant that none of us really had the chance to develop an ego that was greater than the other two.' And, as regards the ingredients of the film's success, director Danny Boyle summed up the recipe from the start. 'We wanted to give a slightly fantastical sense to this story so that it was beyond reality. To get you out of that whole social realism thing which bogs us down – and that's because TV is such a big influence on our culture, such a wonderful influence in many ways – but the dominant thing in TV is, Is it real? Is it the truth? Does it work? We wanted to try and free ourselves of that.'

That they had succeeded in these aims was only apparent initially when, a couple of months after filming finished, the rough cuts were ready for viewing in December. Although normally keen to avoid watching rushes, McGregor made an exception on this occasion and it proved to be a significant moment for him. He later revealed, 'I thought it would be an interesting film, but it was only when I saw the first rough cut and I realised what Danny had done with it that I thought, "God! Did we really shoot this film?" Danny's so clever and he's got a great eye.'

Boyle's own reaction was one of quiet surprise. 'It changed every moment of it. It was completely fluid and I thought, "That's stupid, that's irrational, because the thing is fixed. It never changes." But of course it does, because the audience is part of the story and what they bring to it.'

Still, no one really grasped that *Shallow Grave* could be heading for sizeable success until it received its first showing at the 1994 Cannes Film Festival. Having been denied a place in the official festival's programme, it was screened out of competition on 22 May at a fringe cinema. As world premieres go, it was a decidedly low-key affair, attended by neither the film's stars nor members of the general public. Its audience was made up of journalists, film distributor representatives and other executives in the industry – but their reaction was so sensational that extra screenings had to be hastily arranged. By the end of the fortnight Robert Jones, an independent buyer for Polygram, the major international film distributor, had struck a £1 million deal to distribute *Shallow Grave* in America, Britain, France and Germany. And, separately, distribution rights to almost every other conceivable territory were also sold.

It did not prove, however, to be a hit with everyone. For example, it received only lukewarm reviews in the Scottish Press. One newspaper, whilst dubbing *Shallow Grave* 'undeniably accomplished' and describing the acting as 'competent,' then went on to attack the specially-made set for being unoriginal; the plot was scorned for being shot through with a multitude of holes and the pace was so fast probably because, if it were not, the critic claimed, 'the inherent implausibility would sink the whole affair. Mr Boyle,' the review ended, 'can only go on to better things.'

Producer Andrew Macdonald had frank views on such attacks. He lashed out, I think we have been criticised in Scotland for just about everything. But when you see some of the other reviews you think, "Who cares?" It makes them, dare I say it, look a little parochial.' Yet later, on the eve of its UK general release on 6 January 1995, some London critics joined the negative barrage, declaring, in one case, 'The film is a thumbscrew with no screw, an Iron Maiden with no lid.'

But, by a long way, these dissenting voices were to be drowned out by deafening critical applause. The film was hailed as 'a British thriller of great assurance', 'a masterpiece of creepy terror', when journalists enthusiastically reported on it after a select pre-screening a few weeks before its Glasgow premiere on 19 December 1994. In January 1995 *Shallow Grave* took £152,131 of box-office receipts in its opening weekend as well as breaking individual house records at four London cinemas. Says McGregor, 'It was basically a low-budget thriller but we all knew that it had a bit of style to it, that it was really something rather special. Mind you, it was only when it began to win awards that we realised just *how* special.'

In due course *Shallow Grave* walked off with BAFTA's Alexander Korda Award for the Outstanding British Film of the Year 1994, as well as the Best Feature Film BAFTA Scotland Award and the main Hitchcock d'Or Best Film Award at the 1994 Dinard Film Festival in Breton, France. Danny Boyle would pick up the Best Director Award at the San Sebastian Film Festival in Spain. And McGregor's personal breakthrough with this film was confirmed when, with Kerry Fox and Christopher Eccleston, he jointly won the Hitchcock d'Argent Best Actor Award along with the Francs 30,000 in prize money, at the Dinard Film Festival. He was nominated in the same category for the Bafta Scotland Awards, but lost out on that occasion to John Hannah for *Four Weddings And A Funeral.*

All these accolades properly reflect the success, financial and artistic, of *Shallow Grave*. Out of the top ten domestic films for the period from December 1994 to November 1995 it ranked number one, beating the Oscar-nominated *The Madness of King George* and the latest Bond movie *Goldeneye* into second and third place respectively. At the end of the day the film written, produced and directed by first-timers, which cost barely over £1 million to make, would rake in £27 million worldwide and provide a solid basis from which future fame would grow.

Such dizzy heights for McGregor, however, lay far in the distance. The length of time between the end of filming for *Shallow Grave* and its general release – with all the attendant explosion of prominence – amounted to a full fourteen months. Personally he was fully occupied. For he was soon to meet the woman who would become his wife.

In late 1993 he returned to his life as a young, single actor in a fashionable district of London. 'I had this amazing bachelor pad,' remembers McGregor, 'and the things that went on there!' He had retained the knot of close friends whom he had met during drama school days, including Jude Law. Unlike McGregor, Law came from a strictly non-theatrical family and grew up in London, where he attended a comprehensive school. What they had in common, however, was a burning desire from a young age to become an actor and for a time the two young aspirationals shared a flat in the capital. Jude's film debut would come in the 1994 British movie *Shopping*, but his professional profile was destined to remain lower than McGregor's until his acclaimed 1997 performance as Lord Alfred Douglas in *Wilde*. Ewan's other friends were also actors – Jonny Lee

Miller, the Surrey-born star of movies *Regeneration* and *Plunkett And Macleane*, who would co-star with McGregor in *Trainspotting*, and Sean Pertwee, the future star of the ITV police drama series *Bodyguards* and the son of much-loved actor Jon Pertwee. 'We were all living in Primrose Hill for a while, a hard nut of us,' McGregor recalls. 'Inevitably on the rare week we were all together in a year, some large party affair had to happen.'

Socialising, however, would always come second to work for McGregor. Having just completed another busy year he was about to begin 1994 with two separate parts which though small, were quality roles. Both saw him making another return to the world of television and, for a change, playing two completely diverse characters. First he would be joining the cast and crew for the filming in January of the opening episode of a major new four-part courtroom drama series, *Kavanagh QC*.

The series had been created by Central Films managing director Ted Childs specifically as a vehicle for the actor John Thaw, who had made his name in the Seventies playing a tough police inspector in *The Sweeney*. More recently, he had achieved considerable success in his eponymous role as another detective, *Inspector Morse*. This time Thaw was required to play a top London-based advocate, James Kavanagh, who has risen from northern working-class origins. In each of the episodes he would be the defence counsel in four different cases.

McGregor was to portray the defendant, David Armstrong, in the two-hour feature-length film that would kick off the series. Armstrong is charged with raping a middle-aged housewife whilst he was in the family's employ. The housewife, played by Alison Steadman, is a nervous woman who suspects her husband of an affair, Kavanagh believes that the lonely vulnerable woman, with a score to settle, voluntarily has casual sex with personable young student Armstrong and then cries rape to conceal her infidelity from her husband.

As Armstrong, McGregor had to embody an Oxbridge undergraduate with a wealthy father who demands the best counsel to handle his son's plea of Not Guilty. With money, looks and education, Armstrong projects himself from the moment of his arrest as a softly-spoken, polite individual most unlikely to force sexual attentions on a plain middle-aged woman. Throughout the courtroom testimonies and his robust cross-examination by the prosecuting counsel he remains unflinchingly convincing, leaving the viewer unsure of his guilt until the very end. The sting in the tale emerges after Armstrong is found not guilty; Kavanagh then learns from a young woman in the public gallery that his upright, decent client had been lying all along.

McGregor once more had the part of the villain, this time as a wolf in sheep's clothing. The episode, called *Nothing But The Truth*, would be transmitted on the ITV network at 8.00 pm on Tuesday 3 January 1995, just three days before *Shallow Grave's* general release and its accompanying public recognition for McGregor. But *Kavanagh QC's* creator, and series producer Chris Kelly were already aware of the young star's potential.

Says Ted Childs, 'Because it was the first episode of a brand new series, we were all anxious to assemble as good a cast as was possible in television terms. I had seen Ewan's performances in *Lipstick On Your Collar* and then in *Scarlet And Black* and I rated them both. It was not just my decision, though, but also the producer's and director's. But we all felt that we needed someone young, handsome and plausible. Someone who could convey the impression we wanted of being really nice at face value but who was, underneath it all, a rather nasty piece of work, and Ewan carried this off most impressively. Among the young actors available, we felt that he was the best and as it turned out he served the part well.'

Producer Chris Kelly wholly endorses this view. 'We were thrilled to have him and he was wonderful in the part. He is a committed actor, highly professional and a joy to have around.'

The filming took four weeks at locations in London and elsewhere. Ted Childs recalls, 'We built the interiors which are used as the barristers' chambers, but the exterior shots were taken at Inner Temple which we felt was rather impressive. For this episode the interior courtroom shots were filmed in Oxford.'

It was while shooting these scenes that Chris Kelly felt McGregor really made his mark on the episode. 'The undoubted highlight of Ewan's performance was when we had some trouble in Oxford, when a large crane wouldn't work and we lost nearly a whole day of filming. In television, episodes are shot to very tight time-scales and because of the time lost due to this faulty crane we were really up against it. The scene we had to do was the vital cross-examination by Geraldine James [the prosecuting counsel] of Ewan in the witness box. It was something like eleven pages of script, but they did it in one take. And not only that but because of this pressure they brought immense dramatic tension to what was, anyway, the key scene. We all held our breath while it was happening and marvelled afterwards at what they had achieved, and that was besides being immensely grateful.'

Probably McGregor was the only person present who was not surprised at this display of consummate professionalism. With his rapidly filling store of experience to add to his unswerving faith in his abilities, he now emitted a very tangible, almost daunting, air of self-confidence. Chris Kelly remembers, 'He has this incredible belief in himself and the strangest thing about it is that he is genuinely modest with it. He had excelled as David Armstrong and it was perfectly plain to me that he was going to be a star. On the way back from Alison Steadman's house one day, I told Ewan so.'

Filming for this pilot episode of *Kavanagh QC* would come to an end towards the beginning of February, but not before McGregor had met someone who would rapidly become very special to him. She was a French-born set designer on the programme, Eve (pronounced Ev) Mavrakis. Slender, dark-haired and beautiful, she was well read, well travelled and fluent in a number of languages, the latter gift proving a decided advantage in her work behind the scenes in television and film. She was also around five years older than McGregor – but there was an instant attraction, certainly on his part. Till now he had revelled in his footloose status; still only twenty-two years old, and a rising star, he could have been forgiven for wishing to play the bachelor field a bit longer. But lately he had recognised a kind of emptiness creeping into his otherwise exciting life. He has since revealed, 'I wasn't very satisfied with it any more and then I met Eve and it really did feel very, very different. I knew from the first day I saw her.'

In just over eighteen months' time his conviction that she was the woman for him would culminate in their marriage, followed in due course by the birth of a baby girl. Along the way the Press would be quick to remark on their pairing, dubbing them the latest 'drop-dead gorgeous' celebrity couple on the scene and rating them as rivals in these stakes to Hollywood's Melanie Griffith and Antonio Banderas. With domestic bliss and family life awaiting him McGregor was happy, in the perennially shifting and uncertain world of an actor, simply to have met Eve before he moved quickly on to the second of his new television roles.

Not content with carving international success as an actor, over the years McGregor would take a deeper interest in the whole concept of movie-making, to the point of joining with others to set up a new and ambitious British film production company. And this keen interest in acting at all levels meant that, while he had his sights set on starring in a range of films, from small independent movies to international blockbusters, he also had enthusiasm for what was now an almost extinct art form: the short; a mini-film lasting not much longer than ten minutes.

McGregor waxes lyrical on this subject. 'The short has become an odd thing out, which is a shame. A props master on *Shallow Grave* directed a short called *The Last Ten Minutes*. It went out in a lot of cinemas before *Shallow Grave* – as a B-movie, if you like – and it was brilliant. I remember how nice that was. You've got to make your short film to be seen and to get into the industry. There has to be that opportunity for talented people.'

The opportunity on this particular occasion arose when, in 1993, Lloyds Bank and Channel 4 Films had collaborated to mount a competition challenging young first-time writers between the ages of eleven and twenty-five to come up with an eleven-minute film featuring only three characters and set in no more than two locations. The response was overwhelming with over 2,500 scripts entered, among them one from an eighteen-year-old from Yorkshire, Matthew Cooper. His film, *Family Style*, became one of the six winning entries. And these six would form the first series of The Lloyds Bank Film Challenge Shorts, to be screened on Channel 4.

As a strong advocate of any scheme that nurtures young film talent McGregor was more than pleased to be involved in *Family Style* when the production company Compulsive Viewing began work on Cooper's film, under the aegis of experienced producer Madeleine French. McGregor was cast in the lead role of Jimmy – a choice which at first dismayed the young writer. Says Matthew Cooper, 'I had no part in the casting, but one day they told me Jimmy had been cast. They were very excited. I said, "Who's going to do it?" And they said, "A young Scottish lad called Ewan who's just completed a feature film that was awaiting release called *Shallow Grave*." I asked what else he'd been in and the casting people mentioned *Lipstick On Your Collar*. I remembered him from that, hair slicked back and handsome, not at all the character in *Family Style* – so I had my doubts.'

His unease began to be allayed shortly when the cast and crew began assembling in early February. Cooper recalls, 'Justin Chadwick was brought in to direct, a former actor in his twenties who had played the lead in *London Kills Me*. I had never met him before but Maddie French was brilliant at bringing like-minded people together. Justin was very enthusiastic about the script and after seeing his excellent award-winning short *Walking The Line*, I was convinced that we were going to make a great film.'

He continues, 'Justin Chadwick was very excited about all the cast, particularly Ewan. I was still having visions of him in *Lipstick On Your Collar*, all confidence and cool. Then the day before shooting began I was taken to Boston Spa to meet the cast. I walked into the pub with Justin and there sat Ewan looking exactly like the Jimmy I had imagined and to top it off, he was drinking a pint of best bitter! He was really in character. I joined him in a pint but was too in awe to speak. He was already dressed for the part and had long unkempt hair like Jimmy. He also pointed out a few spots on his face and proudly said he was sporting them for the role. When filming started, though, I overheard the producer telling make-up to "cover up the fucking zits!" '

Cooper was on set for the whole three days of the shoot. Although, after meeting McGregor, he had felt happier about his suitability to play Jimmy, it was only when he had the chance to watch McGregor on set that he finally relaxed. 'Watching Ewan work was a revelation for me. He had tremendous energy and confidence. I was just eighteen and while I was confident about my script, I had never met anyone so confident about what they were doing as him. He was right there in the moment, with no distractions. He was focused and driven to get Jimmy, as I had written him, onto film. I didn't want to talk to him too much, as I thought he needed time to concentrate his mind between takes. But he was great and we had a laugh and a joke. Despite the effort he was putting in, I think he was having fun with the role.'

Making *Family Style* proved to be a memorable experience for McGregor, who came away very impressed with the short and with real respect for Matthew Cooper. 'This guy is just driven to write and if it wasn't for something like this, he would never have been found out, unless it was years down the line when he finally plugged through. This was an incredibly nice way in for him, a great window.' He went on. 'It's a really intense learning process for both the writer and the director. You're being shown the way and helped out by people who know how it works, but you don't have to adhere to anyone. You're just doing it because somebody likes your work.' In this case the proof of just how much McGregor liked Cooper's work came when he used *Family Style* as a calling card. 'I've never had a showreel as such, but I was so proud of the short that I showed it to a lot of people. It's been really useful to me.'

Channel 4 screened the six-part series on Wednesday nights from 11 May to 15 June 1994; the *Times* singled out *Family Style* as one of the most haunting pieces of the series. As McGregor moved onwards and upwards he did not forget the talented young Yorkshire writer, who has since sold a screenplay to British Screen/Miramax. Cooper recalls the encouragement he received from McGregor. 'A couple of months later, he rang me up and told me to keep writing. It was the best phone call I've ever had, especially because by that time the advance buzz on *Shallow Grave* was building.' He adds, 'I knew Ewan McGregor was going to be a big star – and he knew it too.'

CHAPTER 5

Agony and Ecstasy

BY LATE SUMMER 1994, from portraying an obnoxious opportunist who ends up with a suitcase of drug money, McGregor moved over to playing a rootless, good-for-nothing drug-pusher when, exactly one month after *Shallow Grave* broke cover in Britain at the Edinburgh Film Festival, he found himself on the Cornish coast ready to start work on the set of the Skreba Films Limited movie *Blue Juice*. This film has been dubbed 'Britain's first surf movie' and is a quirky comedy examining the meaning of life for a local surf king and three of his friends. For McGregor this would be his third feature film, his second in a co-starring role and the first time he had the opportunity to act opposite Sean Pertwee, one of his closest friends.

Blue Juice had a similar early history to that of *Shallow Grave* in that it had been in the making for a couple of years in the early 1990s before Carl Prechezer, its director and co-writer, and Peter Salmi, co-writer and producer, approached Channel 4 Films with the idea. Again it was David Aukin who picked up the project. Says Peter Salmi, 'David Aukin, Channel 4's Head of Drama, just turned to my co-producer Simon Relph, "godfather to half the British film industry", and asked "And do you surf, Simon?" ' Salmi went on, 'For our debut feature Carl and I wanted to make a character-driven comedy about life for the late-twenties generation in Britain today. We wanted a setting that would give the audience a roller-coaster ride along the way.'

That setting began taking shape in St Ives where Skreba had set up their production office on an industrial estate and where, under slate-grey

September skies, the cast began arriving to commence filming. McGregor arrived on the second day. Producer Peter Salmi maintained, 'Carl and I congratulated ourselves on assembling not only a talented but also a wonderfully good-natured bunch of actors.'

As it happened McGregor had almost been left out of the loop on this particular project, as director Carl Prechezer recalls. 'We had already cast Sean Pertwee and, I think, Peter Gunn, and the strange thing was that although I knew Ewan's work on television and that he was coming through, in the sense that his was the hot name on everybody's lips, when the casting director wanted Ewan, whom I remembered from *Scarlet And Black*, I immediately said, "Don't you think he is too young?" The casting director pressed me saying, "But you really should meet him anyway", which I did. The thing that really struck me was his boundless energy. He has a real buzz about him and that was what shone straight out for me.'

'It was to be a feelgood movie and the tempo was always intended to be jaunty. Some actors are perfect for dramatic roles but not so good in lighter, comic pieces. Each require a different mentality and a different technique altogether. Ewan has both. He came in together with Steven Mackintosh and it just clicked.' The harmony between the cast only improved through rehearsals. 'I put the guys up in the same house during the rehearsal period,' admits Prechezer. 'My thinking was that this was a film about the relationship between all these mates and that can be tricky. You can put some people together to portray this kind of thing, only to find that it just doesn't come off. I realise that it could have hugely backfired, making them live together, but in fact they became so friendly that they would prefer to go off surfing together instead of working and I had a job on my hands dragging them back to rehearsals.'

That this inspired piece of group casting translated into a lighthearted shoot is confirmed by actor Robin Soans who had a cameo role in *Blue Juice* as Farmer Bob, a local yokel who broadcasts a spot on the fictitious Smuggler FM radio show. 'From the start there was very much an all-round unassuming attitude to making the film and this came primarily from Carl Prechezer, Peter Salmi and Simon Relph. They believe that the underlying thing is that it should be fun and they very much passed this on to the cast and crew.'

For McGregor it was also the most lightweight film he had yet appeared in, although his character Dean Raymond is a shifty London drug-dealer, living constantly on his wits. Trafficking in various illegal substances, he cockily declares at one point, 'I know what I'm doin'. Good stuff for my mates and flu pills for the punters.' Once again McGregor had drawn the tougher, short straw; playing the disaffected, outwardly unlikeable villain. His acting range was never narrow, but in these early roles a pattern had already begun to emerge. He played the disreputable Raymond by emphasising the brashness he had projected as *Shallow Grave's* Alex Law, underpinned this time by a nervy, fidgety energy and he laced this latest performance with brief but illuminating hints that he could, after all, possess some redeeming features.

Raymond, with record producer friend Josh Tambini, (Steven Mackintosh) travels together with another friend Terry (played by Peter Gunn), from London to Cornwall to look up their old mate JC. With his surfer's motto of 'One Life, No Fear', and recovering from a back injury, JC is a local legend: he has surfed the treacherous stretch of water known as The Boneyard. Sean Pertwee's JC is approaching thirty and suffering an early mid-life crisis. The four friends, plus JC's girlfriend Chloe (Catherine Zeta Jones) each undergo personal crises, during which they question their lifestyle and seek ways to change.

McGregor arguably had the toughest time of all when it came to engendering the viewer's empathy. Terry finds himself fearful of committing himself to marriage; JC is scared of no longer being a surf idol; Josh is merely guilty of intolerance towards the talents of an earlier generation of musicians. Yet Dean Raymond, just days in town, passes off harmless pills as Es to the local dope addicts; feeds the unsuspecting Terry with Ecstasy for a laugh; steals money from Josh after having secretly sold the story of the record producer's affair with a married recording artiste to the tabloids. He also damages JC's prize surf board. Raymond spends much of the latter part of the film with a battered face, ostracised as a loser. In desperation he again tips off the Press about an attempt to surf The Boneyard, only to take on the challenge himself. His inexperience means he comes to grief, but is saved by JC. In the final fall-out, McGregor's character is redeemed; he begins to earn people's respect.

It is hard for any actor to make the viewer care about the fate of a character such as Dean Raymond. But McGregor achieves this with impressive authority in his performance in *Blue Juice*. 'For me the moment Ewan really stood out,' reveals Carl Prechezer, 'was when Dean Raymond wants to get his life sorted out. I felt Ewan handled that extremely well and it was an important moment. You need a bit of depth in even the lightest film and he projected that. By the time the film progresses Ewan had almost imperceptibly turned his character from being a basically dis-likeable guy to someone who, if you couldn't actually like him, you still *hoped* he could change.'

These deeper strains were deceptively wrapped in a generally frothy tone: with scenes of Sean Pertwee capering naked but for a sock adorn-ing his penis; Catherine Zeta Jones with a penchant for smearing cream over her lover's body to the strains of Marc Bolan's *Get It On*, with the mix of music, drugs and surfing, *Blue Juice* was clearly a film designed to appeal to a young audience. It proved to be an enjoyable experience for all concerned with making it.

Says Carl Prechezer, 'To start with we had the luxury of being able to get as close to the real thing as possible during rehearsals and those days on the beach were invaluable, much more profitable than sitting in some rehearsal room in Soho. It turned out to be quite a tough shoot in some respects, with a six-day working week for about seven weeks. It was my first film and with the schedule changing all the time because of the weather it didn't leave me with as much free time as I would have liked. But still we all managed to socialise, usually in the Sloop public house in St Ives.'

Carl Prechezer goes on, 'There was one brilliant moment when David Aukin and Allon Reich from Channel 4 Films visited the set. As they arrived, Ewan, Sean and Peter were coming in the other direction up the pier, shouting at the top of their voices, "We love this job!" – which was funny because we had just been out at sea in a boat and the weather had suddenly closed in. The boat nearly sank and we had to turn around and come back, having filmed absolutely nothing. It was good to see they enjoyed the job, even on a day when nothing had been achieved.'

The director's final verdict on McGregor's performance was a decided thumbs-up. 'To a certain extent Ewan had an extra task,' he says, 'in that he was rather young to be convincing in the part. Some actors are the age they are and that is that. But Ewan played his youth to his advantage, so much so that it didn't matter if you weren't particularly convinced that he was approaching thirty.' And Prechezer adds, 'There was one glaring difference that I found between Ewan and other actors of his generation and that was that he is very focused and very technically proficient. He understands the grammar and nature of film-making extremely well.'

Blue Juice was released in Britain the following September. Robin Soans remembers, 'People tried to give the film an intellectual gloss which was never intended.' It was certainly deemed by some critics to be somewhat chaotic, but even so it attracted good reviews. The *Express* called it 'an enjoyable oddity', and *Variety* weighed in with the view that it was 'absolutely charming, unabashedly offbeat'.

Its energetic pace had well suited McGregor's personality, it had been very much in keeping with the sense of urgency now pervading his professional life. The mechanics of working in television can aggravate some actors, who feel that the cameras used, which glide around containing actors in one spot, place restrictions on freedom of expression and interfere with the creative process. But not so McGregor. He was keen to seize any opportunity to revisit any medium to explore new horizons – if it gave him another chance to see himself on screen.

Whilst filming *Blue Juice* he had grabbed just such another opportunity; on Sunday 16 October 1994 *Doggin' Around* had been transmitted. Earlier in the year he had joined others to film this one-off drama for the BBC's Screen One season under director Desmond Davis and producer Otto Plaschkes. *Doggin' Around* was written by Alan Plater, the award-winning British screenwriter who has written extensively for radio, television, theatre and film. It was shot in a variety of locations, including Southport, the Pennines and Manchester Airport, as well as in and around London. 'The spine of the plot,' says Alan Plater, 'surrounds a legendary American jazz pianist who comes to Britain for a tour over five nights of the north of England.'

The cast was headed by American star Elliott Gould as the once-famous pianist, now on the skids as the result of drink, women and gambling. The drama reunited McGregor with Geraldine James, with whom he had worked on *Kavanagh QC*. As in the courtroom drama, McGregor's role, as double bass player Tom Clayton, was, once again, in reality an unpleasant character – but one who, this time, *does* come unstuck.

Producer Otto Plaschkes was most impressed with McGregor's professionalism. 'Ewan behaved like a dream on the picture and was a joy to work with,' he said, sentiments more than echoed by writer Alan Plater, who recalls, 'I was delighted and slightly surprised that he was to be in *Doggin' Around*. Surprised because he was already zooming and the Tom Clayton part was strictly subsidiary to the main leads. And the part itself, though nicely written, I like to think, was a kind of smart alec who gets his come-uppance in the final reel. It's subtly done. I don't lay it on with a trowel – that's not my style.'

Plater, who often attended the shoot, goes on, 'Ewan played Clayton as what is called "an educated Northerner" and there was one particularly treasured moment early on. That was when Ewan, in character, first meets Elliott Gould. He says to him, "We never miss the chance to play with old timers." And Gould retorts, "In my neighbourhood we prefer to say 'living legend'." From the start theirs is a combative relationship. But it was the tone of delightful and charming contempt that Ewan was able to direct towards Elliott's character that struck me. He gave Tom Clayton the exact shades and nuances required, with a lovely touch of insolent charm. He taught himself to *look* as if he could play the double bass by dedicated practice and he held his own in pretty fast company. Aside from Elliott and Geraldine we had class actors in Alun Armstrong and Liz Smith, both of whom have the knack of making others disappear: what used to be called "the Denholm Elliott syndrome". Ewan is a fine professional who works hard in the rehearsal room and is good fun on the set. He loves his job and takes it seriously.'

Indeed McGregor, having already won the admiration of so many fellow professionals, had lost none of his laser-precision focus on his career which, as Alan Plater remarked, was steadily shifting up a gear, opening up whole new worlds to him. What he finds most exciting about acting is that it provides a forum in which he can expand his mind and experience. 'You get to portray all kinds of people,' he says. 'I would get terribly bored if I was playing the same kind of character all the time.'

He also gets extremely impatient with those who have made the mistake of seeing him as straitjacketed in certain roles. He bluntly recalls, 'I've had meetings with directors for films where they go, "You know, this part isn't like who you played in *Shallow Grave*. Will that be okay?" ' To which he says his response, if only mentally, is, ' "Fuck off! What the fuck are you talking about, you prick? That's my job. It's what I do." ' Unsurprisingly he maintains, 'So I don't work with people who say that.'

In a crowded and competitive multi-million pound industry, dominated by high-powered agents and advisors who protectively steer their actor-client's every move, McGregor would remarkably keep a firm grip on his own reins. He explains, 'If you're a movie star at my age in Hollywood, agents mainly think they can get you $3 million for a picture and they wouldn't let you do a movie for lower – say, if you really wanted to do a low-budget film with your mates. Now, I wouldn't give anyone that kind of power over my choice of films.' Ultimately he also prides himself on his own instinct being his best compass, even when it has led him into roles in unexpected films. He maintains, 'It's all about stories. It doesn't matter to me when or where they are set, as long as there is a good tale.'

One such tale which appealed to him drew him from filming *Blue Juice* straight to his next assignment and would occupy him in Europe and Asia for several weeks during the coming winter months. If *Blue Juice* would be considered by some as an oddity, this new project was distinctly bizarre, even for an art-house film. It was to be called *The Pillow Book* and would be McGregor's first movie as the solo male lead. It would also provide him with a positive surfeit of new experiences.

His interest started with his reaction to the script. 'It was a fantastic movie script. It was like reading the most beautiful thing, so descriptive. Reading it was a kick in itself,' says McGregor, mirroring the intense passion for the project felt by the film's director, Peter Greenaway. Greenaway's own interest in this project was initially stimulated when he read the original *Pillow Book*, the private journal of Sei Shonagon, who had been a lady-in-waiting to a Japanese empress around the year 995.

Art-house film director Peter Greenaway – whose film credits include *Death In The Seine*, the stylish but brutal 1989 movie *The Cook, The Thief, His Wife And Her Lover* and *The Baby Of Macon* – already had a strong reputation for extreme individuality in his approach to film-making when he decided to tackle a film based upon the writings in this ancient journal. To him *The Pillow Book* was not so much a movie as a visual poem, an extraordinary mixture of weird sexual delights and Japanese calligraphy. His introduction to the original book had taken place when he read Arthur Waley's English translation in the Sixties; thirty years on he had taken the two real-life figures behind *The Pillow Book*, the journal's writer Shonagon and its twentieth-century translator Waley, and turned them into his two lead characters, Nagiko and Jerome, to be portrayed by actress Vivian Wu and McGregor respectively. 'These reincarnations meet, make love and end up writing on one another's bodies. They endeavour to turn themselves and each other into much loved books,' explained Greenaway.

The Pillow Book was to be Peter Greenaway's most erotic film to date. Set in modern-day Hong Kong, it revolves around Nagiko. Whilst growing up, her father had often painted birthday messages on her face: as an adult she takes this practice to new and voluptuous heights, seeking a lover who is prepared to write on her naked body. When bisexual Jerome enters her life he, in turn, persuades her to express her amatory feelings on his flesh, which she does, intending that her writings will be read by her homosexual publisher. There is a sinister reason, however, for the heroine's bizarre fetishes: an elaborate plot to take revenge on her publisher. As Jerome, McGregor plays a highly sensual intellectual whose charged involvement with Nagiko makes him an unwitting participant in these plans. He said of his character, 'Jerome is a complex and vain man. He shamelessly uses and manipulates the publisher and really surprises himself when he falls madly in love with Nagiko.'

What McGregor later dubbed a mad plot but a simple film would prove to be a challenging and richly erotic slice of Asian culture. Heavily dominated by visual imagery, it is a tale in which the overriding concerns are sex and death, power and revenge. Greenaway made effective and innovative use of multi-screen technology to embroider his story; audiences simultaneously viewed the live action alongside woodcuts from the original journal superimposed on the screen. Ultimately it would be hailed as a visual masterpiece that was ravishing to watch. For Ewan McGregor it was the most sexually explicit role of his career to date.

The part of the English translator is short on dialogue and long on sex and sensual scenes. He spends the majority of the film nude, and full-frontal at that. 'This was a very different experience for me but I found it very stimulating. I regularly spent between two and four hours having calligraphy applied all over my body – very sensual and something I will not forget in a long time.'

The film was shot in Japan, Hong Kong and a Luxembourg studio – of the latter location McGregor complains, 'It was fucking freezing cold.' He explains, 'For the calligraphy sequences I went into this cold studio at four in the morning and lay on a bed with heaters at each side. I lay on the bed for two hours while they painted my front and often fell asleep during it. Then I had to stand for two hours while they painted my back, which became a bit tedious, but it was a beautiful film to make.'

The actual process of filming presented a few surprises for McGregor, not least because a lot of it was shot with handheld cameras. Greenaway's attention to detail was immense and this impressed the actor. 'It was fascinating to watch Greenaway work,' he says. 'He really is an artist. It sounds wanky, but it's true – he paints with the camera.'

While he enjoyed working with the controversial avant garde director, it was undoubtedly sometimes an unnerving experience. Greenaway's style of directing afforded McGregor a huge degree of unexpected latitude; he found this unaccustomed freedom to be both invigorating and intimidating. He had first been alerted to this potential challenge at script stage, when he was presented with, not lines to learn, but page upon page of description. 'As if he's forgotten to write dialogue,' he says.

This meant that he had to create his own dialogue. In other areas too he had anticipated more directorial control, only to discover a kind of creative vacuum. 'He would set up these big wide shots and I had to act in them for about four minutes. He'd tell me, you come in here and you end up here and the rest of it is just up to you.' The absence of firm guidance could engender a sense of anxiety. 'You don't know where to pitch it, how far to push it,' he admitted at the time. 'I'm terrified to see it 'cos I might be crap.'

When the film was screened at Cannes in May 1996, the unexpected queues to see this distinctly cerebral art-house offering were attributed by some as due to the sex appeal of 'the British Brad Pitt'. So, naturally, on its

UK release a few months later, on 8 November, much was made by certain sections of the Press about the audience studying McGregor in his full-frontal glory. During the movie's publicity round, McGregor bounced into typical form when asked provocatively by a female journalist if the cold conditions whilst shooting in Luxembourg had constituted a shrinkage problem. 'No fuckin' worries there, darlin'!' he quipped cheekily. He was amused by a review which went into raptures over his 'very handsome penis'; when probed over how he felt about exposing himself to such public scrutiny – about his 'old chap', as McGregor has cheerfully referred to his manhood, being responsible for drawing the crowds to a Peter Greenaway film – he gaily retorted, 'I think that's fucking great. More people are going to see a piece of art and if it takes my nadgers to get them in there, then all's the better.'

When filming wrapped for *The Pillow Book* in early spring 1995, McGregor already knew where he was going next. *Shallow Grave* had already gone on general release in Britain in January and had opened in America at the Sundance Film Festival in the same month. It was while fulfilling his obligations with regards to promoting *Shallow Grave* in the US that McGregor was reunited with Danny Boyle, Andrew Macdonald and John Hodge.

McGregor admits that from an early age he had adored the classic black and white films from the 1930s and 1940s. But his fascination with these romantic Hollywood movies, he found, was at odds with the cynical realities of modern-day Hollywood. Marketing and promotion are the key to any film's success, which meant that *Shallow Grave*'s cast were introduced to representatives from various giant studios and trailed endlessly past an assembled Press pack: an experience which seems to have profoundly irritated McGregor. He reveals, 'They had no idea who I was and I didn't know any of them. Inevitably they tell you how fantastic you are and how much they love your work, even though you know they've never seen you in anything. So much of Hollywood is just bullshit.' Real power and visibility for McGregor had yet to happen; he was not yet wise to the sham and pretence of the PR game.

For *Shallow Grave*'s producer Andrew Macdonald the Americans' effusive reaction to the film was remarkable. Even before it went onto the commercial cinema circuit in Britain it had earned back its budget on the international film festival circuit and was fast becoming a runaway world-wide success. Said Macdonald, 'It is being shown a lot in Hollywood and they are going wild about it. The amount of comeback – Who's that designer? Who's the cameraman? Who are the actors? Who's the director and writer? They are coming up with all sorts of ridiculous offers.'

This spate of startling offers fuelled the mounting clamour to a point where director Danny Boyle was being talked of as Britain's answer to Quentin Tarantino: an anarchic 'outsider' who made the transition into the mainstream. But the *Shallow Grave* team were cautious; they held their nerve and did not allow themselves to be swamped by the hysteria. Said Boyle, 'If myself, John and Andrew can keep together, we've got a much better chance of making British films that sell internationally and mean something to our own audience.' He added, 'You've got to say something as well as entertain. I'm not interested in the one thing going without the other.'

The way to do both and also to stay at the cutting edge of film-making had already presented itself months before when they had decided that their follow-up to *Shallow Grave* would be a film adaptation of the 1993 controversial cult novel *Trainspotting* by Irvine Welsh, a bold and graphic account of the drug scene in Leith near Edinburgh in the 1980s. Danny Boyle calls it a modern classic. 'You come across a book like that every ten years. You immediately say, "Let's make a film of it." It's only later that you sit down and think about all the problems.' In December 1994, Boyle, Hodge and Macdonald were already working on the project and could anticipate critics' reaction to it. Boyle said, 'If they thought *Shallow Grave* was tough, I dread to think what they will make of *Trainspotting.*'

McGregor was blown away by the script. He would be the only main cast member to survive from *Shallow Grave* to the follow-up, but at this early stage even his presence was not guaranteed. McGregor revealed later that Boyle and Macdonald had approached him tentatively whilst they were publicising *Shallow Grave* in America; they had just been given the green light, again by Channel 4 Films, to make the movie. 'They gave it me and as usual they were very cagey and said, "Well, you know, we're not offering you it, but see what you think." '

Film director Stephen Frears once famously remarked about actors, 'A good part – it's like sex to them. They can smell it.' And although McGregor, like everyone else, had no way of knowing just how phenomenally successful the role of Mark Renton would prove, he instinctively knew that it was one of those rare parts that occasionally come along and fairly beg to be seized. He maintains that he gave no thought as to what it might do for him career-wise, but when he landed the role he described it as like getting a million birthday presents rolled into one. 'I knew it would be something special,' he declares. 'I was passionate about it from the very beginning. I could not stop thinking about it.'

Edinburgh author Irvine Welsh has written extensively about the drug culture and has earned himself the sobriquet 'Poet Laureate of the chemical generation.' Welsh says, of its manifestation in clubs and on the streets, 'It's almost like a working class bohemianism.' And his street cred among his predominantly young readership was only enhanced by the shockwaves that this chilling debut novel, with its foul language and horrifically descriptive accounts of gang rape, HIV and heroin addiction, sent throughout the literary establishment. It would attract the dubious honour of becoming the most shoplifted volume ever from Edinburgh bookshops. The heavy use throughout of the Edinburgh vernacular would prove troublesome to theatre directors wishing to tackle stage adaptations of the book; watered-down translations risked diluting the whole ethos. This difficulty would clearly need resolving when the cultural phenomenon that was *Trainspotting* the novel became *Trainspotting* the movie. Undoubtedly, too, taboo subjects to be depicted on screen would prove a difficult challenge; not only must they be handled with the right degree of authenticity, but they must be handled in such a way that the film would not be barred from the mainstream market and the chance of international success.

With shooting due to commence that summer, safe in the knowledge that he had in fact been the number one choice for the role, McGregor knuckled down to his preparation for the role of heroin addict Mark Renton. 'Mark's a pretty complex guy,' McGregor said. 'He does drugs and feels that he can make conscious decisions about when he wants them and when he doesn't. I found it a real buzz time for me – very exciting. And, like *Shallow Grave*, it's a five-star writing job.' But he also confessed, 'I was worried about getting him right.' Which, on one level at least was under-standable. McGregor, though set alight by the part and by the script, could find no real affinity with Renton. He freely admitted that he himself was terrified by the prospect of ever being arrested. 'I was never hard enough to do anything criminal and there were never any drugs to experiment with.' He rightly treated with withering impatience the inevitable ques-tions after the film was completed as to whether he had dabbled with heroin in order to experience for himself its highs and lows before taking on the role of the jagger, or needle-user. 'That's such a load of bollocks. I've had to die on screen before, and I don't know what that's like either. I'm not a method actor at all. So to take heroin for the part would just be an excuse to take heroin. So I didn't.' But this lack of affinity in no way diminished his hunger to take on the task. 'I wanted to play him so badly,' he revealed.

To portray the anti-hero Renton, McGregor complied with the film-makers' two provisos for giving him the part. He shaved his head – which strangely accentuated the natural reddishness of his hair – and since, as a dope addict living on heroin, Renton was unlikely to be beefy, he lost about thirty pounds to achieve the emaciated frame that would pitch Ewan McGregor into the limelight as a shivering, wet, junkie pin-up. 'I felt really good that way,' he said, 'really agile and nice.' The physical changes, though, were window dressing. The real preparation took him down new and harrowing avenues of discovery.

The whole concept of junkie chic was something that McGregor admits he was intrigued by in the weeks immediately after he had landed the role. Of crucial assistance to the film-makers and cast in authenticat-ing the druggie elements of *Trainspotting* would be an organisation called the Calton Athletic Recovery Group, based in the East End of Glasgow. McGregor says, 'I think when I got on the plane with Danny to go to Glasgow I still had a wee element of glamour about it. Till I met these people and listened to their stories.'

McGregor's method of preparing for a role does not, as he will admit, necessarily involve a mountain of intensive research and library study. He is much more instinctive, much more hands-on. He had found the script so amazingly evocative and stimulating that he thought about the charac-ter of Mark Renton continually. It is very much an actor's stock-in-trade to observe people in whichever walk of life is relevant to the role they will be adopting; because McGregor knew that he would be portraying a drug addict, he had studied the junkies who congregated at railway stations whilst in Luxembourg filming *The Pillow Book*.

'I didn't hang out with them,' he makes clear. 'I just watched them from a distance. I'd never initiate myself into the group because that would be too embarrassing.' But these quiet observations afforded him the chance to absorb body language. 'I got some physical ideas from them,' he confesses, adding, 'In one of the first scenes [in *Trainspotting*] I used this stooped posture which is an exact rip-off of a guy I saw in Luxembourg.' He then set about researching drugs themselves. 'I started to read up about hard drugs and addiction, crack and smack and all that, because addiction is a problem on its own, regardless of the drug involved.' John Hodge, as a doctor, assisted by his then girlfriend, a pharmacist, carefully explained to the cast the medical effects of various drugs. But nothing really prepared McGregor for the members of Calton Athletic.

The club was founded by David Bryce and is run with help from former addicts. They refuse to use methadone or any of the other heroin substitute drugs; instead, they rely on one another for support through the tortuous hell of withdrawal. McGregor called them 'the most incredibly inspirational people'; any lingering fondness that he may have felt for the idea of heroin chic was utterly dispelled. 'That immediately disappeared. It's a nightmare of a drug and it's a living hell that these people live.'

Director Danny Boyle, for his part, admits to feelings of sinking despair about the project. 'It was really depressing,' he says, 'and we didn't really want to make the film. We couldn't relate to it creatively at all. But then we met these guys from Calton Athletic and that was a pivotal moment. They are fanatical. They say you give up now and never go back on it and if you go back you're out of the group.'

The *Trainspotting* team worked closely with the ex-addicts who were constantly on hand to give advice and insight right down to how to inject and how to convey graphically the nightmarish physical and mental anguish endured whilst experiencing cold turkey. Boyle states, 'They showed us everything. I felt that having them around was enough to make the film responsibly and accurately.'

'I think it would have been a very different film without them,' says McGregor. 'They had one guy, Eamon Doherty, who was on set with us whenever we were using drugs and his experience and expertise in the field was invaluable.'

One stomach-lurching moment that would become notorious occurs in the scene featuring a close-up shot of Renton injecting intravenously into a vein in his arm. McGregor reveals, 'It is my arm but moulded prosthetically and with a plastic pip going into a little pool of blood underneath so you can see the pulse.' Whilst setting up this scene what struck McGregor most was how everyday and ordinary the whole practise appeared to be to Doherty. And in his quest to understand a drug-addict's psyche he decided, 'I think what means everything is what happens after you've put the needle in your arm – everything else is irrelevant.' He went on, 'We spent two weeks with them. Rehearsing, listening, playing football and learning how to cook up heroin. There's a certain mystique about the preparation of heroin that isn't there in reality – it's just a pain in the arse.' For the film they used a mix of flu tablets and cocoa powder to fake heroin being readied for injection.

There was a lot to absorb, and McGregor recalls his first steps onto this steep learning curve. 'I heard Eamon, who ended up being our advisor, tell his drugs life story and I'd never heard anything like it. I'd never felt anything like the atmosphere of support in the room – the giving of strength to each other from these hard men and women. It felt almost religious. But I didn't feel that we were using them, because I don't think that they felt we were. They knew that we were serious about wanting to make the book into a good film.'

Irvine Welsh firmly believed that there was a public appetite for films that showed the underbelly of society. But because his book was episodic, rather than relying strongly on narrative, he had never envisaged that it would translate easily to the screen. Indeed, when he was initially approached to sell the film rights, he confesses, 'I thought it was brave of them.'

Hodge later amplified these hurdles. 'There's a lot of internal monologues, lots of different characters, almost no narrative at all until near the end and the language is quite difficult. I thought it could end up being one of those films that fails to do justice to a great book.' Macdonald and

Boyle, however, were highly persuasive and Hodge agreed to write a workable screenplay. 'You've got a captive audience for two hours. It's about how fast it is, how much action, how much juxtaposition of characters. That's what you've got to deliver.' To this end he concentrated on a small group of characters, with the central protagonist being Mark Renton. The incidents of the plot, when strung together, created a story of 'Rents' and his chance to change. 'The film depicts his philosophy and his nihilistic selfish way of life which aren't particularly attractive traits but at the same time he's charismatic, intelligent and attractive. He's still got a heart, maybe a slightly damaged and bitter one, but he's still a human being.'

What author Irvine Welsh, who would be given a small cameo appearance in the film as a drug dealer, would think of the final screen treatment worried the trio. But Welsh in fact approved of the script. Says Hodge, 'He gave us some notes which were generally positive, with a few minor criticisms. It was great because obviously he could have chosen to be very difficult and precious about it.'

Although the story is set in Edinburgh, like *Shallow Grave*, again filming was to take place in Glasgow. But, unlike Boyle, Macdonald and Hodge's debut film, this follow-up would not be receiving financial backing from the Glasgow Film Fund; its allocated yearly budget for 1995 was already spoken for. 'If *Trainspotting* performs as well as *Shallow Grave*,' predicted the *Sunday Times*, 'the fund could be kicking itself in a year's time.' In fact *Trainspotting*'s budget was a modest one and ended up just over half as much again as *Shallow Grave*'s had been, at £1.7 million. Channel 4 Films invested more money in the project than they had ever previously committed to a single film. Offers of American money had been thrown at them following *Shallow Grave*'s success in the States, but this was turned down because, they said, they 'wanted to keep this one to ourselves'.

Filming for *Trainspotting* got underway in blistering heat as the summer of 1995 came into its own. Although there was a certain amount of outdoor shooting, the majority of scenes were shot indoors. Producer Andrew Macdonald explains that because too many small British films founder due to the pressure of shooting on a tight schedule whilst being at the mercy of an unpredictable climate, they did not want to take the same risk. 'The only way we could make it,' he says, 'especially with 230

ABOVE The stars of *Trainspotting*: Begbie (Robert Carlyle), Diane (Kelly Macdonald), Sick Boy (Jonny Lee Miller), Spud (Ewen Bremner) and Renton (Ewan McGregor).

ABOVE Just two months after its UK release, *Trainspotting* broke through the £10 million mark, becoming the fourth highest grossing British film ever.

ABOVE Nice face – shame about the wig! Ewan's role as Frank Churchill in the period film *Emma* was not his finest hour.

BELOW Peter Greenaway's erotic film *The Pillow Book* saw Ewan and actress Vivian Wu writing sensually all over each other's naked flesh.

scenes in the film, was to do as much of it in the studio as we could. That decision stylistically affects the rest of the film.'

Trainspotting was mainly shot in the spacious derelict building that was once a Victorian Wills cigarette factory on Alexandra Parade. Inside this makeshift studio a collection of sets had been constructed depicting flats and bedsits of various sizes, each displaying differing degrees of squalor.

From its pulse-pounding opening shot of Renton hurtling down Edinburgh's Princes Street to the sounds of Iggy Pop's 'Lust for Life' with two store detectives hard on his heels, *Trainspotting* takes audiences on a kaleidoscopic journey that is sometimes loathsome, sometimes stomach-churning and sometimes funny. Renton is very much the central figure; he narrates in voice-over and the exploits of his circle of friends are largely seen through his eyes. 'Who needs reasons when you've got heroin?' he demands contentiously, challenging the viewer to take on board his philosophy of life. Amidst the drug abuse going on around him, the strength of Renton's own habit is clearly and gruesomely established almost at the beginning of the film when he uses an opium suppository, the loss of which, when his days of constipation come to a sudden and dramatic end, leads the film into one of its most surreal stretches when Renton dives head-first into a filthy blocked toilet to retrieve it.

The love interest is typically quirky: after being seduced by a girl he meets at a nightclub when his sex drive, long suppressed by heroin, returns, he discovers next day to his affront that she is only a schoolgirl. His few scenes with Diane (played by Kelly Macdonald) allowed McGregor's cheeky sensuality to shine through.

For nineteen year-old Kelly Macdonald, previously an out-of-work barmaid in Glasgow, her graphic sex scene with McGregor would be a particularly testing baptism of fire. The seduction scene took, in total, half a day to shoot and Macdonald admitted that her anxieties were so bad that she spent most of the time leading up to the shoot in the toilet. 'It was the scene I was most dreading but you can't suddenly say, "I've changed my mind".' She goes on, 'I didn't have a clue what I was going to do. We'd had rehearsals in clothes but that was just embarrassing.' In the end, according to Macdonald, it was McGregor's experience that got her through it. 'Ewan was great. He kept it all sort of fun and laid-back. He just gets on with it and he's a really good laugh at the same time.'

In the film, driven by McGregor's monologue, Renton comes off drugs only to return to them; he overdoses; he undergoes agonising cold turkey during which he endures unimaginable horrors physically and mentally. The depths of despair experienced are not understated in his harrowing ordeal. In an attempt to change what life has ordained for him he goes to London and finds work as an estate agent but is soon traced by his friend Sick Boy and a local nutter called Begbie, who is on the run from the law. Finally, Renton makes off with a suitcase of drug-dealing proceeds, leaving the others to their respective fates. His ultimate pronouncement, on ripping off his mates, is to say that he is a bad person – but will clean up his act. It's left to the audience to decide whether or not he is truly redeemed – or whether he will be back on heroin before too long.

It is a powerful depiction of an unpalatable but growing section of society and one that was bound to provoke a strong reaction. Most controversially of all, it dared to show the highs as well as the lows to be had from doing hard drugs. Speaking of this during the research period Danny Boyle said, 'You realise how force-fed we are with the image of heroin. You must never speak positively of this drug because it will lead people to use it, and lose their lives. You have all these images that it's like a virus and as soon as you touch it, you're finished. But if you are going to do a film about it, you've got to find out about it. If that doesn't conform to the expected picture, that's too bad. Clearly there is a glamorous side to the drug too. People don't take it because it's going to kill them or because it's going to make them sick. They take it because it's going to make them feel wonderful and you've got to tell the truth about that.'

McGregor was, and remains, a staunch defender of *Trainspotting*. 'I think we showed it the way it is and of course to begin with there's got to be some up side to it, otherwise why are people doing it?' The down side is a very quick spiral and if the film shocked when it appeared to celebrate the enjoyment of drug abuse, it was equally shocking in its portrayal of the degradation that heroin addiction can reduce a human being to. But along the way at no point did it moralise, as most other drug-issue films do.

Over the course of making *Trainspotting* McGregor became acutely sensitised to the whole issue of drug-taking, particularly heroin. 'It's the big bad one. I mean, why is it worse to be injecting heroin into your arm than to be doing a line of coke in a toilet? I suppose socially it's to do with the needle. Your gut reaction to syringes is to recoil in shock and horror – the idea of an implement putting things into your body makes it all seem very clinical and medical and that sets it apart.' And clinical just about sums up his eventual view towards what, when speaking with Eaman Doherty only months before, had been totally alien to him. 'The tools of the trade are so mundane. After doing this film picking up a syringe is like picking up a cigarette.'

Although Renton shoots up, steals and goes through a nightmare withdrawal, in such an exaggerated, in your-face movie he is in reality the calm centre in the eye of the maelstrom of dirt, drugs and violence. Much of the time the action happens around him, this can make actors uneasy and McGregor was no exception. Not long into the shoot he realised that there was not much for him to actually do in many of the scenes except watch. 'I panicked. It's the hardest thing about acting. I think Danny knows that. Having a nervous breakdown, screaming and shouting is the easiest part. Actors fuckin' love doing all that, never happier than when they're crying their eyes out.' He voiced his concerns to the director and was assured that that was unavoidably the way it had to be. Boyle later said, 'There's a lot of difference between not doing anything and doing nothing. Renton is very modern. He doesn't show much emotion. He becomes what you want him to be.'

If McGregor's underlying fear had been that, because of a perceived lack of opportunity, he would fail to shine, it was unfounded. He was already a master of conveying a great deal by doing very little. According to actor Jonathan Hyde, with whom McGregor had worked on the film *Being Human*, this quality was innate, not simply a matter of technique. He says, 'What Ewan possesses is a huge amount of flexibity. He has tremendous energy but also a great capacity for relaxation, which are the two elements that make up a really good actor. One without the other either puts the audience to sleep, or is hugely irritating.' Jonathan Hyde believes that McGregor deployed both these elements in perfect balance in *Trainspotting*. And *Time Out* magazine would also praise him, 'It's what McGregor doesn't do which really hits home.' Robert Carlyle, the future star of the Oscar-nominated comedy *The Full Monty*, was eminently dangerous as the unpredictable, hard-drinking psycho Begbie. Jonny Lee Miller held down the role of Sick Boy, the menacing lady's man with his passion for James Bond movies, whilst Ewen Bremner, who had played the Mark Renton role in the acclaimed 1995 stage version of *Trainspotting* at the Traverse in Edinburgh and at London's Bush Theatre, turned in a sterling, and at times endearing, performance, this time as the vacant-looking speed-assisted Spud. But McGregor always seemed somehow set apart.

Film producer Lord David Puttnam says of McGregor's performance, 'He was amazing. He has terrific forgivability.' And there lay much of the key to McGregor's success as Renton. He may be a drug addict, a liar, a cheat and a thief, but it is his intelligence, humour and the sheer attractiveness of his amorality which persuade the viewer to like him in spite of their better instincts. Boyle likens McGregor to Michael Caine in this capacity and certainly Renton's voice-over is as sharp and charismatic as that of Alfie's in the 1960s blockbuster of the same name. McGregor himself said of his character, 'I quite like him – but I don't like the fact that he's given up on everything.'

When shooting on *Trainspotting* ended in mid-July 1995 McGregor was both proud and possessive of what he felt to be wonderful work. However, he does believe that in *Trainspotting* a number of very good scenes were eventually sacrificed at edit – sent to the cutting room floor. 'For whatever reason, good or bad,' he says, 'from the beginning they were intent on making it exactly ninety minutes long.'

Still, he had loved every minute of making the movie, although often he had found it mentally and physically draining. He cites the scene in which he and his mates discover that a baby belonging to one of them has died. 'That's a very demanding, horrible, emotional scene, but then that's quite a challenge and a kick as well.'

McGregor had had only two afternoons off during the whole seven weeks of filming but he was uncomplaining; he had adored working once again with the trio he affectionately called 'the Three Amigos'. 'They could all be working in America,' he said. 'But they came back to Glasgow to make a film about guys on heroin. They're risky geezers!' A particularly good rapport between director and actor can make an immense difference to a film and the harmony between Boyle and McGregor this time around, on their second project together, had been sublime. Boyle described his leading actor as 'a thoroughbred. You get them once in a while.' To which McGregor quipped, 'Maybe he means I'm fast and skinny. Maybe he thinks I'm in-bred – thin ankles and skitty.' But the experience further deepened an already burgeoning mutual admiration society.

Trainspotting would become a bench mark in McGregor's fast accelerating career, a fact not fully appreciated until the film's release. Making it had been hugely rewarding creatively; his sense of exhilaration had been such that he might now have experienced a let down had he not had a different kind of rush ahead of him. Having just completed what would become the most important film of his professional life he was, within only a couple of weeks, ready to take the most significant step of his personal life when at the age of twenty-four he married his girlfriend Eve Mavrakis.

The wedding took place at the end of July, in the lush green valley of the French Dordogne. They had borrowed a house belonging to agent Jonathan Altaras for a week; it had an extensive garden, complete with swimming pool. Over the course of that week family and friends – sixty people in all – gathered and in due course the marriage ceremony took place in the town hall of the small village of Festalemps, officiated over by the local mayor. McGregor wore a pale suit; the cultured Eve Mavrakis wore a chic sleeveless dress. Disappointingly for McGregor his uncle Denis Lawson was unable to attend due to stage commitments, but it was a special and memorable seven days. It was a refined yet relaxed affair from start to finish. 'We all cooked for each other at nights,' McGregor reveals, 'and drank fine wines in the garden. It felt like absolutely what we wanted to do. That's very unusual when you have a dream, to actually see it totally realised, which our marriage was. It was perfect.' He admits that he had never imagined marrying so young but he also confesses, 'The second I saw Eve I thought, if I could be with her, it would be like nothing I've ever had before. I believe I'll be with her for ever and that we'll go through everything together. Otherwise I wouldn't have got married.'

The lot of a busy actor, however, meant that, just as he had had to attend his wedding still sporting the skinhead style of Mark Renton, so he was soon to be prized away from his marital idyll into his next film. He was due to go on set within a fortnight of his marriage. It was to be a role which was as far removed from the Edinburgh junkie as could be imagined – and one which, for the first time in his career, would cause him some problems. The incredible pace of his career was now about to start stretching him in ways that he had not yet experienced; and unfortunately, as far as he was concerned, his latest career decision would turn out to be a mistake.

Trainspotting

McGREGOR'S HEAD–SPINNING days of fame got off to a negative start in August 1995 when, from his real-life married state, he returned to eligible screen bachelordom in a big-screen adaptation of the Jane Austen classic *Emma*. 'It was really difficult. One minute I was lying on the floor with a syringe in my arm, then I got married, then I was standing in this trailer with a wig and top hat and leather gloves on and for a moment I thought, "I can't go from skinhead drug addict to ha-ha-ha curly wig acting".'

McGregor is not one of those actors who excessively immerses himself in a role. 'I do think there's almost an element there subconsciously,' he once ventured. 'For example, when I was playing Alex in *Shallow Grave* I was quite rude to some people and I think I was slightly more aggressive than I normally am when I was playing Renton. When you're concentrating on certain aspects of someone else's personality, it brings your attention to these aspects in your own character. But I don't have to *live* a character.' The problem was not that Renton had taken over his mind to such a degree that he could not easily exorcise him, but rather the rapidity of the turnaround he was expected to make. For any in-demand actor such speedy transformations are par for the course, but this was McGregor's first taste of having to carry out two startlingly opposed characterisations in such quick succession. In the future he would prove both his versatility and his ability to transmute successfully and swiftly from one character to another, but in this instance, as he will admit, he came unstuck.

The screenplay based on Austen's novel for the Matchmaker Films Production movie had been written by Douglas McGrath, recently Oscar-nominated for his screenplay, co-written with Woody Allen, for the 1994 movie *Bullets Over Broadway*. With *Emma* he was also making his directorial debut, teamed with producers Steven Haft and Patrick Cassavetti. Shooting took place mostly on location in Dorset in the summer of 1995. The central characters were the eponymous heroine, played by the Californian-born actress Gwyneth Paltrow, and Mr Knightley, handled with neat understatement by Jeremy Northam, well cast as the forthright, handsome hero. They were supported by an ensemble that included Alan Cumming, Toni Collette, Polly Walker and Juliet Stevenson. McGregor's role was that of one of the more minor characters, Frank Churchill.

The story revolves around the tangled machinations of Emma's incessant matchmaking schemes on behalf of various friends and the late discovery of her own heart's desire residing in Mr Knightley. Frank Churchill is the son of the man who has newly married Emma's former governess and his character's arrival in the fictional town of Highbury has been much anticipated among the ladies.

McGregor makes his entrance midway through the two-hour film. Driving her horse and trap into a deep ford Emma has become wedged when Churchill, appropriately enough on a white steed, canters into view to assist the damsel in distress. Regretfully this type of genteel period role had never particularly appealed to McGregor 'I've read a lot of period adaptations and most of them bore me to death in the script form.' With an aristocratic accent, he looks and sounds uncomfortable in *Emma*. Whether he is attending a ball; a picnic; saving a young lady from assault; or ultimately thwarting Emma's romantic plans for him by being secretly engaged to another girl, he never looks comfortable, at ease.

His performance was also hampered by other considerations. Although it has been claimed that McGregor is six feet tall, he looked a touch dwarfed in his scenes with the swan-necked Paltrow. Visually there was another drawback – his wig, something that became much commented upon. Coming straight from a skinhead role he clearly required a hairpiece to play the dandy but the shoulder-length blond wig with its side-parting did nothing for his looks. Producer Ros Anderson, who had worked with McGregor on his last period production, *Scarlet And Black*, called it 'downright cruel' on someone's part to have landed the actor with such an unattractive specimen.

Nevertheless, the blame for the below-par performance did not lie entirely with the cosmetics. One reviewer would remark that he had hoped Frank Churchill's much-vaunted arrival in *Emma* would inject some backbone into the staid proceedings – but that was not to be. 'It comes to nothing,' he stated, 'as does his part, in the end.' A blunt assessment against which McGregor puts up no argument, although the actual process of making the movie pleased him well enough in some ways. He considered that the script was witty and fast-paced. By singing a duet with first Emma and then his secret fiancée Jane Fairfax (Polly Walker), McGregor got the chance to flex his vocal chords – always something he enjoys. He appreciated too, being allocated a big on-location trailer for the first time. And although period costume was as always restrictive, it had its compensations. 'All actors like dressing up, regardless of what they might say. It's fun, all that stuff. It's so different.' He also derived particular pleasure from working with some of his fellow cast members. 'Toni Collette was brilliant, so funny and such a nice person. And there was Jamie Cosmo who played my dad in *Trainspotting* and played my dad in *Emma* as well.'

But otherwise *Emma* turned out to be a dismal experience for him. 'The wig had a lot to do with it. Also the accent. We were forced into doing this very clipped proper English accent. So, as a result, I wasn't really talking to anyone. I was just trying to sound right.' He continues, 'I think the film's all right. But I was so crap. I was terrible in it. I didn't believe a word I said. I just thought, "Shut the fuck up, Frank!" It was the first time for me. I was really embarrassed about it and I'm not paranoid about that usually. But this time I didn't know what I was doing.'

Emma was to be screened first at the same Cannes Film Festival as *Trainspotting*, in May 1996. It was shown at a gala dinner – $25,000 a table – hosted by Hollywood doyenne Elizabeth Taylor together with Cher in aid of American Aids charities. When it was released in Britain and America, it did well, going on to secure an Oscar for its music as well an Academy Award nomination for Best Costume but none of that prevented it from attracting criticism. Derek Malcolm of *The Guardian* wrote, 'The whole thing gives off a pungent smell of antimacassars, fatally weakening the hard-nosed sense of reality Austen possessed. This is the way to make a heritage movie but it is not the way Ang Lee went with *Sense and Sensibility* and it is why McGrath's effort, able in other directions, is comfortably outshone by his.' McGregor came under specific fire for some especially inane facial expressions, with one journalist memorably describing him 'grinning like a game show host.' Barry Norman said, 'He was miscast in *Emma*. It was certainly Ewan McGregor on a bad hair day – the wig definitely did him no favours, but he isn't particularly right for costume drama. He has a contemporary face and uses contemporary body language.'

McGregor himself had a highly contemporary view of his own performance when asked how he felt when he first sat down to view the film. With bald honesty he volunteered, that as far as cringing went, 'I was under the fucking sofa!' But he was not yet ready to crawl away into a dark hole in shame. He was rescued by his famous india rubber resilience and his embarrassment soon evaporated. The freedom to experience the occasional failure in British acting is something he cherishes – something from which an actor can learn. 'If you miss and hit the wall every now and again it doesn't matter. Failing is important too.'

As usual, when filming on one movie was over, the fortunate McGregor had another project lined up. His next role would take him up north; having gladly ditched his upper-crust tones he would now be required to convey a convincing Yorkshire working-class vernacular – something he was a deal more comfortable with. His new movie was to be called *Brassed Off* and it was soon apparent that it would become a fine example of British films at their grittiest, street-level best.

Put together by Film 4, Miramax and Prominent Features, the film, like *Shallow Grave* and *Trainspotting*, was an ensemble piece. It focused on a small group of people, each well-drawn characters and each with their own problems, connected by the biggest threat ever to their financial and family security during the brutal series of enforced and politically-motivated coal mine closures in the early 1990s. Written and directed by Mark Herman, it brought together a very strong cast of considerable experience and talent in the shape of Pete Postlethwaite, Tara Fitzgerald, Philip Jackson, Stephen Tompkinson, Jim Carter, and Peter Martin.

McGregor was the youngest of the group and, leaving nineteenth-century dandy Frank Churchill far behind, he was immediately at home as Andy Barrow, a miner, one of the lads, whose future hangs in the balance.

Herman's first feature film as writer/director had been the 1992 Warner Brothers movie *Blame It On The Bellboy*. The comedy had starred Dudley Moore and Patsy Kensit but had been condemned as instantly forgettable: *Variety* magazine declared, 'ingenious plotting is let down by weak dialogue and stop-go direction that largely squanders the talent involved.' The exact opposite would prove to be true of *Brassed Off*.

Herman centred this story on the closure of a profitable pit in the fictional town of Grimley. As a Yorkshireman himself he knew his subject and crafted a film of memorable quality from start to finish as it conveyed, in parallel with the struggle against redundancy, the fate of the pit's brass band and its attempt to reach and win the national music finals at London's Albert Hall. In real life the legendary South Yorkshire Grimethorpe Colliery Band had lifted the winners' trophy just as its members' pit was shut down and their livelihoods were ruthlessly torn from under them; *Brassed Off* was to be filmed in the town of Grimethorpe, a once proud community which bore the scars of understandable resentment – a resentment which some of its citizens came to direct at the film crew. One newspaper reported the need for the production company to tighten its security measures after receiving threats of firebomb attacks. But none of this prevented the cast, including McGregor, from sympathising with what they encountered there during filming.

'It was almost like Beirut,' Philip Jackson recalls. 'Iron shutters clamped down on everything to stop people being robbed and kids as young as five running around after 11.00 pm. The actors did all integrate into the community, which I think helped, and mostly it was good, but the town's deterioration had its downside. The local pub by about midday had a regular group of people who were already pissed out of their heads and sometimes they wouldn't be very cooperative about being quiet while we were filming nearby. The town is such a sad place. One woman told us that if anyone had said to them a few years before it happened that the pit would close, no one would have believed it, it was such a prosperous place. And she started crying.'

Another cast member, Peter Martin, confirms, 'Oh, the situation was not good at all and the locals were pretty hostile towards us at first. I think they thought that we were there to take the piss out of them and they got up to some naughty things. It is a rough area. Now their reaction is different. They'll happily say things like, "Ewan McGregor played pool in here," and so on, but initially it wasn't easy.'

Easy or not, filming commenced in October. As Andy Barrow, McGregor spends the film, when out of his bandsman uniform, dressed drably – a complete contrast to his appearance on arrival in town. 'He dresses weird,' says Martin. 'The first time I met Ewan he was wearing a bright orange jacket and bright orange trousers and I thought he was a council worker. I asked him, "Where're you digging up today then, son?" He took it in great part though.'

McGregor himself called *Brassed Off* 'a very passionate film about the destruction of a community'. He eagerly knuckled down to work on his role as the young coal miner who plays the tenor horn at night for the colliery band. His own training on the French horn helped him to – as he put it – 'tootle along with the tunes'. Says Philip Jackson, 'Ewan was better at it than the rest of us. I'd done something like this before years ago and I can read music so I got a bloke in the real band to write out for me which finger was used for each note and that way I managed okay. Peter Martin, my sidekick in the film, didn't bother. He just blew any old note.'

To perform the actual music and to help those like Martin who had not a clue how to *look* like players, professional help was on hand from the Grimethorpe Colliery Band members, one of whom was Malcolm Clegg. 'For the scenes in the rehearsal room players of whichever particular instrument sat close to the actor who was supposed to be playing that instrument. Tenor horn players sat next to Ewan in case he needed any help. The most fun we had was with Pete Postlethwaite – trying to educate him into being able to conduct – but overall the whole thing was a nice experience. Ewan got on well with everyone, particularly Philip Jackson, Peter Martin and Jim Carter, and his character, Andy, brought a few old friends to mind for me.'

Besides being one of the musical miners, McGregor provided the romantic interest, his leading lady this time being Tara Fitzgerald who plays local girl Gloria Mullens. She works for the mine's management who are trying to close the pit down; although she tries to keep her secret, McGregor is quick to blow her cover.

In a departure from many of his scenes with leading ladies in the past, this time there would be no nudity; a kiss on the lips in the presence of his rowdy friends is as raunchy as it gets. McGregor's most telling scene comes in a low-key yet emotionally charged moment when Andy and Gloria meet and talk after the pit has closed and she, by now unmasked by his friends, is apparently leaving town. 'Look, for years, bloody years, nowt good's ever happened to me,' he tells her. 'The only reason I get up in the morning is to see if me luck has changed, but it never bloody 'as.'

Of the earnest young Andy, who declares himself as having no hopes, only principles, McGregor explained, 'He's in a desperate situation and is genuinely trying to hold on to the final threads of optimism. But it's an uphill struggle.' His performance totally conveyed the hopeless dejection of the young man and held a fascination all its own. He had his moment and seized it. The director confirmed, 'He's very restrained. He hardly moves. But you watch him all the time. He has amazing eyes. You can tell so much through the eyes. Isn't that what makes a movie star?'

McGregor continued to command respect as an actor from his older, more experienced co-stars. Says Peter Martin, 'Ewan is a lovely young man and very talented. It was clear that he was going to go far and he's such a heart-throb to the girls.'

Philip Jackson adds, 'In one way it was difficult for Ewan having this juve lead role, and the story line with Tara was slightly extraneous to the main theme, but he handled it well and it worked. His accent was good too and he was very easy to work with – a lot of fun.'

The seven week schedule was hard work but the cast did make time to socialise. Jackson recalls, 'The colliery scenes were done at a working mine near Doncaster and for the whole shoot we were put up in a hotel in Doncaster itself. It's from there that we mostly went out on the town a lot. Ewan likes his beer and is a superb pool player and we had a lot of laughs.' The laughs, though, definitely did not include fooling around with girls. He might have been a 'heart-throb' in his professional life but McGregor, just four months' married, was no longer a ladies' man. Indeed he was already well on his way to becoming a father; Eve, who would become accustomed to going on location with him, was already some months' pregnant.

The overtly fearless political message in *Brassed Off* would play a vital part in the movie's strength and appeal. For McGregor, already alive to social and economic injustice, these overtones struck a definite chord. He described the movie thus, 'It's a really brilliantly political piece of film-making,' adding that it was a cracking people's movie, very moving and very passionate. The blight caused by the pit closure to the town of Grimethorpe especially distressed him. 'I saw three-bedroomed houses for sale for £5000,' he said; 'people desperately trying to get out of there. I was there for seven weeks and, at the end, I was just so saddened by it all that I was dying to get away.' He added, 'I hope the people there like it, because we're telling their story really.'

When *Brassed Off* went on general release in Britain on 1 November 1996, as McGregor hoped, it won votes of approval from those locally involved. Peter Haig, secretary and treasurer of the Grimethorpe Colliery Band says, 'I was at the colliery till it closed. That film is part of my life. It just hits you. The story is so real to me.'

Commercially too it gave no cause for complaint, although after the phenomenal success internationally of *The Full Monty* – another British film with a similar, if more subtle political subtext – many feel that *Brassed Off* didn't receive the recognition it deserved. Barry Norman believes, 'I think that what perhaps worked against *Brassed Off* was its overtly political comment. Personally that's one of the things I most admired about it. But a lot of people don't like or want such strong political stances in a film. Any pill can be swallowed if it's sugar-coated.'

The kind of instant recognition that came McGregor's way as 1996 dawned was the sort most actors normally only dream of. The springboard to success that he had sought from the start, not many years before, finally and dramatically arrived with the UK release of *Trainspotting* on 23 February. Polygram had been determined to help it become a smash hit and it was essential that it took off big in Britain first. To this end the distributors were prepared to plough £800,000 into the film's promotion. 'We're treating it like a blockbuster,' Polygram's managing director Peter Smith said prior to *Trainspotting*'s release. 'It won't make it anywhere else if it isn't a hit here.' The belief began to grow that it could be a cross-over movie, that it could appeal to a much wider audience than the obvious core youth market, and predictions looked likely to be fulfilled when the clamour which had been building since a preview screening just weeks before, reached new heights.

The film wasn't without its detractors. In Scotland the *Herald* felt, 'Beneath the flashy direction, the speed, the stylish editing, the clever set designs, there is nothing at all except a monster hit. It is a lot of sound and fury adding up to a Chinese meal.' But most critics hailed it a break-through movie. *Variety* dubbed the cinematic portrayal of British delinquent youth 'a *Clockwork Orange* for the Nineties'. The *Independent* declared it 'a blistering roller-coaster of a movie that mines a rich vein of black humour.' And against a backdrop of similar effusions – some com-plimentary to the point of drooling – the director, producer, writer and cast were plunged into the cyclone of a media frenzy.

Whatever McGregor expected, nothing he had so far experienced had prepared him for being smothered by a never-ending stream of journalists and photographers jockeying ferociously for his attention, lining up inces-santly to ask the same repetitive questions in a blinding and bewildering round of non-stop interviews. And this was just the start. With the movie due to show at Cannes in May and its American release scheduled for the summer, he could look forward to this brand of bedlam for months ahead.

The media seemed to have an obsession for analysing every aspect of the motivation behind the film. Danny Boyle repeatedly explained, 'I think it's about trying to cover the territory that is normally a kind of real-ism in British films and actually trying, through humour and tone, to lift it out of that realism which can often be a bit prosaic.'

Andrew Macdonald reinforced the director's point. 'It's not about social realism. It's a buddy movie.' He added, 'It's about a group of men – their friendship, loyalty and betrayal.' But for most critics, it was about one thing and one thing only – hard drugs. Their seductiveness and destructiveness. Feature after feature made famous Renton's line in the film when he describes the unrestrained joy of a heroin hit: 'Take the best orgasm you've ever had, multiply it by a thousand and you're still nowhere near it.' This helped fuel what became a raging debate: whether *Trainspotting* danger-ously glamorised drug addicts and drug abuse.

Prior to the film's release McGregor seemed to be bracing himself to handle the noisy controversy. Danny Boyle called Renton 'the audience's intravenous vein into the film'; having the pivotal role it was natural that McGregor would be relentlessly singled out by the Press and called upon to defend his views. Answering the complaint that Mark Renton was being dangerously portrayed as a youth hero of the 1990s McGregor maintained, 'I never thought that. He doesn't give a shit about anyone.' And whilst, perhaps, not particularly keen to set himself up as an all-purpose spokesman for the generation, his standpoint on drugs was realistic. 'If someone's constantly telling you. "Don't do this. Don't do that," especially as a kid, the first thing you want to do is go and do it. It's much more responsible to say, "It'll make you feel fantastic for a short while, but then it will lead to this, this and this." '

A brief respite from promotional interviews came on 15 February when the film's world charity premiere took place simultaneously at Glasgow's Odeon cinema and at the Cameo and UCI cinemas in Edinburgh, with a percentage of the proceeds going to the Calton Athletic drug rehabilitation programme. Those involved in the film spread their attendances around. Novelist Irvine Welsh joined John Hodge and Danny Boyle in watching the film at the Cameo, whilst across town Andrew Macdonald turned up at the UCI. McGregor managed to put in appearances in both cities.

The Edinburgh events had started nearly ninety minutes before Glasgow's scheduled show to enable people from the capital to make it along the motorway for the post-premiere bash for 800 guests to be held afterwards at the Briggait centre. McGregor therefore spent time at the UCI before heading west to Glasgow and Renfield Street, where hundreds of celebrity spotters had been out in force on the pavements outside the Odeon for hours before the evening showing, straining at crush barriers to catch a glimpse of McGregor and other cast members.

Having been touted as the most eagerly anticipated British film for years, tickets for *Trainspotting*'s charity premieres sold out in ninety minutes in Glasgow and in a third of that time at Edinburgh's Cameo cinema, which was taken as a sure sign of the film's assured success. This was confirmed when advance bookings for the movie's regular screenings, to begin when *Trainspotting* went on general release the following week, were

ABOVE The stars of *Brassed Off* line up proudly with members of the Grimethorpe Colliery Brass Band at the back of London's Royal Albert Hall.

ABOVE Tara Fitzgerald provided the love interest for McGregor in *Brassed Off*.

OPPOSITE PAGE Not only a talented actor, Ewan is consistently rated high in the heart-throb stakes!

LEFT Ewan's meteoric rise to fame culminated in him landing the biggest role of his career in *Star Wars*.

BELOW Ewan enjoys an extremely close relationship with his family; here he is pictured with his father Jim and grandmother Phyllis Lawson at the 1998 Highland Games in Crieff, Perthshire.

unprecedently high – certain to smash individual house box-office records.

On emerging from the premiere not everyone was bowled over. Scots writer Peter MacDougall, responsible for some hard-hitting television dramas, was quoted in the Press later as saying, 'It's got nothing to do with drug-taking, nothing to do with violence. It's all to do with hype.' But in answer to those few who predicted that the massive hype bubble would burst and the film would quickly disappear, the first in an impressive string of box-office statistics quickly demolished this claim when, just two months after its UK release, *Trainspotting* broke through the £10 million mark, seizing the distinction of being the fourth highest grossing British film ever at the domestic box office. And the surprises had only just begun.

Films steeped in controversy are shunned when it comes to securing nominations in mainstream movie award circles. But *Trainspotting* would go on to win a number of prestigious prizes, including the BAFTA Scotland award for Best Feature Film. McGregor would also pick up BAFTA Scotland's Best Actor accolade. For the second year running he would land the *Empire* magazine award for Best British Actor and he would also collect the prestigious Actor Of The Year award from the London Film Critics' Circle. John Hodge, meanwhile, would make off not only with the BAFTA Best Adapted Screenplay honour but would also lift the coveted gold-plated Oscar in the same category the following year.

The film's general release only engendered further heated debate over the issue of glamorising drugs. Barry Norman was one of those who did not see it that way. He says, 'I totally disagreed with the calls that this film glamorised drugs and drug-taking. I thought it did the very opposite. If you take the baby's dying scene. If anyone could watch that, then go out and start sticking needles into themselves, they would have to be depraved. Unless someone was already an addict – in which case it would be a waste of time – that single scene alone out of many would put people *off* drugs.'

Someone else who voiced an opinion was Janet Betts, the mother of Leah Betts, the teenager who had tragically hit television headlines when she died after taking an Ecstasy tablet at her eighteenth birthday party. 'Our older daughter watched *Trainspotting* and said that it put her off drug-taking for ever, that its depiction of what can or will happen was so diabolical that there was no way after seeing it that she would ever enter into anything. It made a lot of people think, but I can also see that there is an element out there which would find it all a big laugh. I do feel there is a need to show more realism – these things *do* go on – but the trouble, for me, was what happened after the film, after the book, and then there is a follow-up book. That's when the danger of glamorising it comes in, I think.' She adds, 'Film-makers do have a real responsibility to be very careful. In *Trainspotting*'s case I am split right down the middle. I think that they did some good, but I also believe that they did some bad.'

The strength of the row perplexed McGregor. To him *Trainspotting* was, like all films, a reality taken to extremes. He contended that shooting up heroin was not as extreme as blasting someone in the face with a gun, a commonplace sight in mainstream cinema. 'Heroin is obviously not a good thing, as you can see from what happens to several characters in the film. But also, we're not saying these characters are evil bastards, that only evil bastards do drugs. I don't think this film will promote heroin use at all. Unless people are very stupid.'

With the hype in overdrive and showing no sign of slowing McGregor managed to detach himself from it to some extent as the film did the round of Britain's cinemas – he was due to leave the country. 'Apart from doing all the Press,' he said, 'I missed the buzz. But I'm delighted it's been so successful. I was passionate about it and it's a nice reflection of my taste that people think it's good as well.'

One of those people was film director Carl Prechezer. He says, 'This was probably Ewan's most stand-up performance, and again it was the way in which he handled it with his energy and the depth he gave it. What Ewan has an abundance of is zip. He truly has the ability, too, to make you really want to watch his character on screen . . . to care about what happens to him, even when his isn't a particularly likeable character. A lot of actors would have played Renton in a much more internal way, and that would have been interesting in its own way. But Ewan's approach, exuding this raw energy, was definitely the way to go.'

Despite – or because of – the controversy *Trainspotting* would reportedly gross around £350 million worldwide. And amidst the firestorm of attention engulfing everyone involved with the film McGregor quickly emerged as the key player. Although posters were made featuring each individual member of the main cast, it was invariably Renton's stooped body and suffering face that stared down from innumerable billboards and gazed gauntly from magazine front covers. It was practically impossible to move and *not* see him, to pick up a publication and *not* read about Ewan McGregor.

Trainspotting was the film that sent his stock soaring. But as Ewan-mania kicked in for the first time, McGregor himself took flight, literally, escaping from the madness at home to the relative sanity of filming thousands of miles away in Los Angeles where he was about to make his US film debut. A prospect which, despite his newly bolstered self-confidence, still filled him with a certain sense of awe.

Terror, Tears and Temper

'LIKE THE WORLD'S biggest caravan park' is how McGregor ingenuously described his first glimpse of Los Angeles as he pressed his nose to the aircraft window. He was flying into the City of Angels to start work in mid-March 1996 on a decidedly ungodly film called *Nightwatch*, for Dimension Films. The contemporary thriller was a remake of a 1994 Danish hit by writer/director Ole Bornedal who had gone to Hollywood in the hope of duplicating his European success. A grisly slasher movie, it told of a serial killer on the loose in the city, murdering prostitutes and each time leaving his signature on the corpse by gouging out their eyes. McGregor was to join forces with Patricia Arquette, Nick Nolte and Josh Brolin to commence work under Bornedal.

It was the first film in which he had had to adopt a convincing American accent. McGregor's was the lead role, Martin Belos, a law student working part-time as a mortuary night watchman who swiftly becomes the prime suspect for the gruesome crimes. Its Scandinavian success made McGregor query about the director, 'I wonder if he just directed the same film again?' With its many plot twists and turns, *Nightwatch* was peppered with red herrings to spice up the already chilling mix of weird sexual practices, including sadism and necrophilia. McGregor, getting his teeth into the part whilst absorbing everything about this new experience, particularly admired both the sets and his fellow cast members.

There was one noticeable difference, however, in working with American stars rather than British actors and this became evident quite quickly. McGregor recalls, 'I think that in Britain we tend to learn the lines and just say them the way that the writer wrote them. Whereas in America, actors seem to be more like jazz musicians. They act around the line and ad lib their way through. The writer's word isn't all.' As in *The Pillow Book*, this sort of freedom isn't necessarily something with which he feels comfortable.

Nightwatch was shot in Los Angeles on a two-month schedule, fortunately not so tight that he was unable to take some time out both to enjoy the sunny weather and to indulge in his penchant for buzzing about on motorbikes: an avid enthusiasm which he found he had in common with co-star Josh Brolin. McGregor was the proud owner of an old '74 Motoguzzi and whilst in California he eyed up a powerful Harley Davidson, much tempted to fly it home to London when filming was over. As the world's epicentre for movie-making, the sprawling, humid and star-packed Los Angeles is considered to be the most licentious and tempting city in the world where power is the ultimate goal. It usually makes an overwhelming impact on eager young actors during their first trip there, but, recovering quickly after his breathless touchdown in the film industry's mecca, McGregor discovered himself to be an exception to this rule.

He is adamant that it is not important to him to crack America. 'Break into what? A system of bad movies?' he has asked, maintaining that he is content to select from the many scripts that flow to his door. If the best ones happen to be filmed in Hollywood, only then will he go to work there. 'That's all it's about, that town,' he regularly states. 'It's only for making movies; there's nothing else.' And to stick around in the city after the process had ended would lead, he maintains, to loss of creativity. 'I couldn't live there. In this valium lifestyle, you'd quickly lose critical faculty,' he declares. It was therefore no surprise that, as soon as he had fulfilled his filming commitments on *Nightwatch*, he hightailed it back to London.

Nightwatch was due to be released in the US as early as late 1996, but in fact it did not open in the States until April 1998. Poor reviews precipitated its withdrawal from cinemas and it was sent to video ignominiously fast. (It was released straight to video in the UK six months later.)

McGregor might not have been enamoured of the Hollywood system but at least he had come away from his latest project with a decided buzz.

He had particularly enjoyed working with Nick Nolte, the Oscar-nominated star of *The Prince of Tides* and *Jefferson In Paris*, whose renegade streak makes him a colourful and unique figure in Hollywood. And the simple fact of having made his US feature film debut held its attractions for McGregor; it could be seen as another milestone marker in his career. Speaking later that year he described himself as an actor who could not be better placed. 'I feel so incredibly lucky and blessed,' he declared. His reason for feeling so blessed that spring was more personal, for on 4 February 1996 his wife Eve, after a twenty-four-hour labour, had given birth by Caesarean section to a baby girl.

Ewan and Eve had had to rush out of their London flat in the early hours of the morning to the hospital where Clara Mathilde McGregor was eventually assisted into the world. For McGregor it was a profound experience. 'I wasn't prepared to be that frightened,' he admitted. The length of time for which his wife was in labour increasingly worried him, and systematically undermined his determination to be strong for her. He has called it the longest emotional experience of his life. When it was decided that a Caesarean birth was the best option, he was with Eve. 'All I was thinking was, "Oh no! I'm not big enough for this, not quite sure if I can handle this one." ' But he did handle it, and has since stated how extraordinary it was. 'That's something you can't put into words,' he says.

Not long after the birth he was on the telephone giving his relations and close friends the happy news, crying with relief and delight. He was, and remains, the proudest of young fathers. When he trailed alone, bewildered and dazed back to his empty apartment, which bore all the tell-tale signs of a hasty evacuation, his world seemed to have suddenly shifted permanently on its axis. 'You can never go back now,' he mused.

But going backwards had never been McGregor's style. Nor had standing still. His bankability was steadily on the rise and Press speculation had claimed his fee for *Nightwatch* to have been half of Nick Nolte's reported £1 million pay-off. While he had been filming in Los Angeles speculation had continued to mount as to whether, now that he had tasted Hollywood, he would be lost to Britain. Film pundits would repeatedly ask McGregor if he adhered to the accepted wisdom that, when all's said and done, to succeed on the bigger stage British actors must desert their own film industry for Tinseltown. McGregor erupted. 'I don't care enough about breaking into America to give a shit about it.'

But, as *Brassed Off* director Mark Herman stated, 'It's all there for him, if he wants it,' adding, 'I hope he stays.' McGregor himself acknowledges that the lure is strong. 'It's made very tempting for you to leave,' he admits. 'But I'll go and do films wherever. I don't see the problem with going to do a film in America then coming home. *Nightwatch* was the same deal, the same process. The technicians wore bigger toolbelts and I suppose the star system is slightly more extreme in America – but that is the only difference.'

He also frequently asserts that it is quality work he cares about and not money, nor what the public might necessarily consider shrewd career moves. He would prove the truth of these words on two occasions in the coming seven months by taking time out to appear in a walk-on part in a television drama and by starring in a short film as a favour for a friend. The walk-on part was in *Karaoke*, screened on BBC 1 over four Sunday evenings from 28 April 1996.

Karaoke, the work of Dennis Potter who, dying of pancreatic cancer, had depended on the relief provided by morphine-heroin cocktails in his pain-racked final weeks so he could complete his last two plays, *Karaoke*, and its sequel, *Cold Lazarus*. Poignantly Potter had observed, 'My only regret is to die four pages too soon.' Between April and June the BBC and Channel 4 TV – at the playwright's dying request and in the first joint venture of its kind – simultaneously screened these two plays.

Karaoke, directed by Renny Rye and produced by Kenith Trodd and Rosemarie Whitman, starred Albert Finney and Julie Christie. Like *Lipstick On Your Collar* the drama was again semi-autobiographical. It revolved around a writer who is convinced that the fictitious characters he is creating are actually coming to life. But, unlike *Lipstick On Your Collar*, McGregor had no more than seconds on screen: his cast listing is merely as 'young man'. But he had much admired Potter and his courage. It meant a lot to him to do the part, as Roy Hudd, who also co-starred in *Karaoke*, recalls. 'When I played Albert Finney's agent, Ben Baglin, the opening scene was me picking up Albert from a hospital. As we got into my car a young couple walked by. The boy had one line to say. Albert heard the one line and said, "It's a line from my film." The start of the plot really. The director called "Action!" and the young couple walked on – the lad was Ewan. He'd turned up to do just that one line as a thank you to Dennis who had given him his big break. Nice.'

There is proof aplenty that McGregor, despite his burgeoning fame, feels genuine affection and respect for those with whom he has worked along the way. Roy Hudd gives a classic example of how McGregor is not shy of showing this. 'The last time I saw Ewan was at an awards ceremony in 1997. He had to read some nominations, then clips from the nominated films were shown. While they were being shown Ewan suddenly leapt off the stage, came to our table, lifted me up and gave me a big hug while announcing to the room, "This man is the greatest!" Even if I'm not, it was a smashing thing to do.'

Such naturally unaffected exuberance in what is anyway a highly demonstrative profession could scarcely fail to further endear McGregor to his peers, very few of whom begrudged him his jet-propelled career, the highspot of which came zooming back sharply into focus once more when *Trainspotting* hit the 1996 Cannes Film Festival. Its strong subject matter kept it out of contention for the coveted Palme d'Or Award, but it was instead given a special screening. Its first foreign premiere took place at a midnight matinée in the early hours of Tuesday 14 May 1996, at the vast Festival Cinema. McGregor had flown in to Cannes with Macdonald and Boyle by private jet; the stampede among the assembled Press for interviews created pandemonium.

He later reflected, 'It was a trip. We made quite a noise.' A somewhat ironic reference to spending an entire five-day stretch coralled in a room with a hundred or so representatives of the world's media, intent on raking over the same old ground concerning the drugs question. According to McGregor he was rendered near dribbling by the end of his hectic stay at this annual frenetically chaotic and glitzy gathering in the French Riviera. He was certainly flat-out exhausted the day after *Trainspotting*'s post-premiere party, a celebrity bash held at the sumptuous Palm Beach centre on the Croisette promenade. It was *the* party in town and as such attracted guests of the calibre of Oasis star Noel Gallagher and Rolling Stone Mick Jagger.

Trainspotting fever had again kicked in. It would reach new heights of delirium with the film's American release on 19 July – in anticipation of which the film's powerful US distributor Miramax was insisting on what one newspaper termed an 'obscene amount' of Press promotion. Amid the hype the call to compare Danny Boyle with director Quentin Tarantino gained fresh legs – a cry with which Barry Norman takes issue. He says, 'Danny Boyle put together quality in *Trainspotting*. He did a splendid job. But in content or in anything else there is no real resemblance to Tarantino's work.'

For his own part Boyle focused on his film's upcoming launch into the American market and it seems that he entertained serious reservations as to how it would perform there. Doubtless much of this was due to concerns that Americans wouldn't be able to understand a word of the broad Scots dialect even after, to make it more accessible, specific parts of the dialogue had been re-recorded.

But any fears of failure would quickly vanish as the deluge of publicity for the film began in advance of its Stateside premiere. For McGregor this meant a positive avalanche of profiles on him personally in most of the country's major publications. Whilst he had been in America earlier in the year shooting *Nightwatch* the set had been regularly invaded by the US Press on the scent of interviews for *Trainspotting* – the fruits of which were now glowering out from front covers and cramming the New York newsstands.

The film's New York premiere would be a benefit event for a music industry Aids charity. On its opening weekend in a three-day span on only eight screens it grossed $262,673, which meant that it chalked up the highest earnings per screen in America that weekend. It drew rave reviews in the States too, along with in inevitable storm of criticism from the US anti-drugs lobby.

Despite this Miramax tried to promote comparisons to a much earlier event when a film concentrating on four British young men with strong regional accents made the transatlantic leap big time. Dutifully some reviewers, picking up on this cue, attached to it the label of '*A Hard Day's Night* for the Nineties'. But it was hopelessly incongruous to compare the clean-living image of the Beatles in the mid-Sixties with the drug-ridden amoral characters of *Trainspotting* thirty years on. Quickly another handle sprang up in tandem as the movie was ambitiously advertised as 'Britain's answer to *Pulp Fiction'*. For any film the only answer that matters is the one which refers to box-office receipts and when *Trainspotting* went on general release it took New York by storm. Its distributors went on record by stating that they anticipated they would take $20 million in America. In fact *Trainspotting* would treble that figure and then some.

Trainspotting's US release came while McGregor was on the other side of the world in the far more tranquil environment of the Republic of Ireland, already two weeks into filming his latest movie. A determined Press contingent had pursued him to the Emerald Isle intent on laying siege to him at the film set, but McGregor had by now said everything there was to say about the heroin addict Renton and the drug culture. He preferred to concentrate on his role in the seventeenth-century mystery thriller, *The Serpent's Kiss*.

Almost twelve months before McGregor had found it a bizarre and ultimately disastrous experience moving from Eighties skinhead Renton to a long-haired Regency dandy in *Emma*. Now, as the spotlight burned brighter than ever on him, he had returned to period garb. But this time he knew exactly what he was doing – and had thrown himself into the role with gusto.

Based upon an original screenplay by Tim Rose Price *The Serpent's Kiss* is set in Gloucestershire in 1699 and is a tale of blackmail, sexual intrigue and deceit. A Jones-Brockmann Production in association with Rose Price Battsek Productions and Trinity Film, filming had originally been planned for summer 1995 but was postponed for a year. Shooting on location around the tiny village of Sixmilebridge in County Clare had begun on 1 July and would stretch over the next seven or eight weeks. McGregor, with top billing, had been cast as Meneer Chrome, a flamboyant and handsome young Dutch landscape artist who is employed by a wealthy landowner to redesign the extensive grounds of his English country house. He joined fellow cast members Pete Postlethwaite, Greta Scacchi, Richard E Grant and Carmen Chaplin to work under director Philippe Rousselot.

Chafing at her dull country existence and coldly impervious to her husband, Julianna (Greta Scaachi) turns her attentions to her husband's virile new employee. Although not immune to the older woman's charms, Meneer's own desires lie more in the direction of her spirited nubile daughter Thea, played by newcomer Carmen Chaplin. Then Julianna's relative Fitzmaurice (Richard E Grant) arrives on the scene. Quickly jealous of his cousin's infatuation with the landscape artist, he blackmails Chrome, over whom he seems to have some hold. Clearly there is more to Meneer Chrome than meets the eye – an intriguing facet which McGregor relished the opportunity of developing. 'I am playing two different levels most of the time – who I am, and who I want them to think I am. It was really interesting to toy with that – sometimes letting it slip.'

The one thing that McGregor had not been prepared to let slip was the part itself. The film's producer Robert Jones revealed, 'This film was a long time getting going and he could have walked a hundred times, but he stuck with it despite very heavy pressures. Everybody wants to work with him.' McGregor, in fact, had found the script to be one of the best he had read in an age. It had vitality; it was peopled by captivating and complex characters. He had committed himself on paper to taking the lead in *The Serpent's Kiss* before *Trainspotting* had elevated him to his new megastar status, but his loyalty to the project proved unshakable in any case. 'I was offered a lot of other films,' he confirmed, 'but I was always going to do this.'

This time round McGregor's preparations had included getting to grips with a Dutch accent. He admitts that he found it difficult initially. 'But the voice coach recorded the whole part on to tape in a Dutch accent,' he reveals, 'and I listened to it constantly for three weeks.' As in *Emma*, he would potentially be constrained by period costume – but instead of starched formality, *The Serpent's Kiss* had an earthy, more natural atmosphere. So, in sharp contrast to the snug-fitting jackets and top hats of Frank Churchill, as Meneer Chrome he had a far more sensual and dashing image with long hair and loose flowing shirts.

As Barry Norman stated, McGregor is a strictly contemporary actor with a contemporary face and body language. However, the makers of *The Serpent's Kiss* deliberately set out to bring a contemporary look and feel to their production. In a deliberate departure from traditional costume dramas, *The Serpent's Kiss* projected, via its dialogue, humour, and to some extent its central themes, a noticeable modern accent. That McGregor was much more at ease than previously became apparent to all on set, especially the costume designer. Consolata Boyle believed that McGregor's distinctive modern image look was a great part of his strength. 'His nonchalance when he wears a costume is exactly what I wanted. He is completely underwhelmed by it,' she stated.

The director Philippe Rousselot also believed that McGregor had brought a distinctive and mesmeric quality to the role. 'There is no recipe for star quality,' he maintained, 'but he's very quick, very bright and with a fascinating face.' He added, 'You can't take your eyes off him on screen. He is among those actors that can display a very wide range of emotions by hardly moving their face. It brings back memories of the great actors from the Hollywood era.'

Considering McGregor's childhood admiration of the old Hollywood legends this was a compliment guaranteed to please him, although by now such plaudits were becoming commonplace. His co-star on the film Richard E Grant, remarking on McGregor's meteoric rise, says, 'It's amazing that his head doesn't turn 360 degrees, but he is astonishingly grounded.'

One of the main things helping him to stay grounded was that Eve and Clara accompanied him to Ireland and stayed with him at his hotel. It was not an uncommon sight on the set to see McGregor walking about with his little daughter strapped into a baby carrier on his back, or pushing her in a buggy shaded against the sun. In his free time he swapped being a doting dad for drinking in the local pub, playing pool and tapping into the rich and evocative Irish music. But the moment he really had the chance to let his hair down was when Richard E Grant staged a big bash during filming.

McGregor later told reporters, 'Richard had been booked into this castle hotel and decided to have a glam rock party. There were 350 people dressed in glam rock gear.' McGregor didn't describe his own outfit but revealed that the host had been resplendent in a shocking pink skin-tight crotchless catsuit complete with a diamante-studded codpiece, with the requisite high-heeled platform shoes, and a silver wig.

If making the film had at times also resembled one big party, the end product still had the power to sober McGregor's responses. Even after his recent tumultous success, he continued in his own words to be 'gobsmacked' to see himself on the silver screen. Two years on he would still be stating, 'I still can't believe it is me up there.'

The Serpent's Kiss would have its world premiere at the Cannes Film Festival in May 1997; it was shown to a muted reception. Its UK premiere took place nine months later on 21 February 1998 at the Glasgow Film Theatre, as part of the Scottish People's Film Festival. It became a family affair on that occasion when his parents and maternal grandmother, Phyllis Lawson, came to lend their support, as did Denis Lawson. But McGregor, cheeky as ever, decided to play a little joke on the Press.

His friend Jude Law also had a movie, *Gattaca*, showing during the festival on the same evening, at Glasgow's Odeon in Springfield Quay. The Scottish Press were out in force for the event. McGregor, Law and their wives decided to swap partners for the evening's socialising. Jude Law arrived at the Odeon with Eve Mavrakis; McGregor turned up at the Glasgow Film Theatre with Jude's wife, actress Sadie Frost. Their aim to cause a stir, however, bombed when scarcely anyone noticed what they had done. Sadie Frost told the Press, 'We thought everyone would wonder if we were having affairs, but no one seemed to bother.'

Provoking Press speculation of an affair was at odds with McGregor's usual fiercely protective attitude to his and his family's privacy. His devotion to his wife and daughter is evident in many ways; one yardstick was his increasing frustration at how limited his free time was rapidly becoming as his workload grew. Days after wrapping up work on *The Serpent's Kiss* he was looking forward to some quality time with Eve and Clara when an afternoon telephone call from Miramax shattered that prospect. The film company needed him back in Los Angeles to reshoot and revoice some scenes for *Nightwatch*. With a mixture of fatigue and sheer disappointment at being robbed of this small oasis of rest, he exploded.

With unfortunate timing a journalist had been with McGregor to interview him and so his first and angry reaction became public knowledge. His incautious outburst was quoted word for word, 'Why didn't they fucking notice this three months ago?' Such was his rage that he refused to be soothed by the Miramax executive's attempts to convey that the extra work would prove to be of advantage to him in the long run. He was out of patience with what he felt was flattery.

McGregor was of course fully aware that reshoots can be unavoidable. He also quickly realised that his outburst might be interpreted as ingratitude. 'People are gonna think, "What a wanker! He should be thanking his lucky stars!" ' he said, adding that he most certainly did appreciate his good fortune. He loved being in demand as an actor – it was just that he wanted a life too. He solved the problem as best he could by taking his family with him when, in mid-September he temporarily returned to the heat and smog of LA.

The eventual negative critical response to *Nightwatch* came as no surprise to Ewan. When the movie's UK release began to be threatened he spoke out. 'This was the perfect example of a film they would not leave alone,' he maintained to one interviewer. 'There were constant reshoots, including the ending, and they took all the interesting stuff out, making it bland. The original concept was the reason I accepted it in the first place. I had massive strands of the character removed, which is insulting.' He obviously felt that his initial reaction to the reshoots was more than justified.

McGregor has also always maintained that 'the money side [of making movies] can get out of hand.' Despite being bombarded with lucrative offers, he put his money where his mouth was in the autumn of 1996 when he found time to appear in a TV short for a director friend with whom he had worked before, Justin Chadwick.

Chadwick had directed him in Matthew Cooper's *Family Style* in 1994. Now McGregor agreed to appear in Chadwick's own twenty-minute mini-movie, *Swimming With The Fishes*. It was pointed out to him, bluntly, that he had no need to do this kind of thing any more; McGregor replied, equally bluntly, that he believed in Justin. Matthew Cooper reflects, 'Mini movies, or shorts, for Ewan, are about working with new people and about the challenge of getting a feature-length performance into a few minutes – big characters into little running times. I think that's what interests him more than anything.'

Swimming With The Fishes is set in a Greek fish-and-chip shop where McGregor's character works. Over-sexed and always on the make, he recklessly fools around with the owner's daughter which lands him in deep trouble with the Greek mafia. He is only saved from certain death by his father's timely intervention when he ingeniously enlists the help of ghosts from the Greek gangsters' past. The five-night shoot involved scenes of noisy semi-clothed sex, and murderous intent at sea; incongruously it took place in Eastbourne. McGregor's sexual appeal was clearly not being harmed in any way by his private married bliss; his co-star, actress Nadia Sawalha, joked, after their simulated steamy sex, that she just might not bother with the real thing ever again. She said of McGregor, 'You can see there's something about him the minute you lay eyes on him. He's dead cool.'

Swimming With The Fishes, which was screened a couple of times in London around the turn of 1997, would signal one of the last times McGregor took part in a television production. His thoughts and energies were already focused on a reunion with the *Trainspotting* team, with whom he had already signed up to make his next film. The prospect of working with Boyle, Macdonald and Hodge for a third time excited McGregor to the core and he was proud to wear his loyalty to the trio on his sleeve. 'I'm never happier than when I'm working with them,' he would declare. He believed that they had taken a big risk with *Trainspotting*, especially as expectations had been raised by the surprise success of *Shallow Grave*. By that measure, then, the risk was greatly multiplied by their decision to follow their global smash hit with a third collaboration which was intrinsically different from either of their first two. Said McGregor, 'They have their ideas, their vision, and they don't allow people to compromise them.'

Trainspotting was still riding high. Danny Boyle, perhaps prophetically, remarked at this time, 'It's really easy surviving the triumph. But it's when we make a really fucking lousy film and survive that . . .' Their ideas, their vision now lay in a romantic fantasy called *A Life Less Ordinary*. And while 'lousy' might be too extreme a description, it would seem that the Midas touch might not turn all it touched to gold this time.

CHAPTER 8

Not So Ordinary

BY NOVEMBER 1996, with the *Trainspotting* worldwide express hurtling on, *Emma* on general release and *Brassed Off* and *The Pillow Book* arriving in UK cinemas within a week of each other, Ewan McGregor was being hailed as Britain's hottest star. The range of his talents was truly beginning to make itself felt. Moreover, on top of this he had, on the strength of Renton, entered the ranks of the Hollywood A-List of actors.

Being the men of the moment Danny Boyle, Andrew Macdonald and John Hodge were all very much individually in demand, snowed under by a shed-load of offers. Macdonald reveals that quite a few of those offers were seriously tempting, especially one for he and Boyle: *Alien 4* with Sigourney Weaver and Winona Ryder. 'The script was great,' he admits: 'But after a few meetings Danny and I realised that it wasn't the kind of film we wanted to do.' McGregor was also being headhunted by swarms of Hollywood executives eager to lock him into a stellar system that can ruthlessly exalt or brutally extinguish a career. When in Los Angeles he had already encountered many a movie mogul only too ready to educate him on the accepted wisdom of selling his soul, metaphorically, to an industry which allows actors to indulge themselves with a couple of independent films – so long as they make the next ten for the giant corporation.

The concept was alien to McGregor and he firmly resisted it. To him the reason to make any movie is to try to produce the best work possible and for that he believed he had to be selective about working with good people. The British film industry – in which he has great faith – was itself developing into a more verdant state than of recent years, and with the help of cash injections via the National Lottery an unprecedented number of films were being funded. McGregor was there smack in the middle of this much-needed push to revive, but he was also only too aware that at the same time financing and shooting a film is not the whole answer. Solid distribution is essential to success, and in this field it is American companies that largely dictate which movies actually make it into the cinema circuit. At least partial US backing, then, was in the main a desirable framework on which to build any film. *A Life Less Ordinary*, therefore, fitted the bill in every respect. It was a project written, produced and directed by the three people McGregor believes to be the cream of film-making talent and as a Twentieth Century Fox film, its $12 million budget was partly American-financed.

According to Andrew Macdonald, 'Sixty-five per cent of cinema audiences in Britain are under twenty-five years old and most film-makers don't consider that. They want to make grown-up movies that will win Oscars. On the whole, I think British film-makers need to be a lot more savvy about their audiences.' *A Life Less Ordinary*'s sheer quirkiness was blatantly intended to appeal to a younger age group.

The seed of the story, according to the film's producer, dated back to around the time of *Shallow Grave*, in 1996, but the final draft of the original screenplay by John Hodge had only been completed in the summer. It was an ambitious attempt at a screwball comedy fantasy set in America. Hodge had actually crafted *A Life Less Ordinary*'s hero Robert with McGregor specifically in mind: a fact that McGregor was unaware of until he arrived on set in Salt Lake City, Utah in November where, over the next three months, the film would be shot.

McGregor was to lead a cast that included British actor Ian Holm and American stars Stanley Tucci, Holly Hunter and Delroy Lindo. The heroine, Celine, would be played by Cameron Diaz, the Californian Long Beach-born model turned movie star who had made her screen debut opposite Jim Carrey in the 1994 Entertainment/New Line movie *The Mask*. 'American actors are what the world wants to see, like it or hate it,' stated Andrew Macdonald, and so he and Danny Boyle had felt it necessary to bring in an American beauty as the female lead. There was no apparent shortage of interest in the post. Earlier in the year, whilst attending the Cannes Film Festival, in the midst of the bedlam over *Trainspotting* Boyle was said to have received interest from one or two famous names asking the director to be considered for the lead role in *A Life Less Ordinary*. As director, Danny Boyle would not be rushed into making a decision and required to give it his serious consideration. The names of other top actresses – Uma Thurman, Winona Ryder – had been floated before they had opted for Cameron Diaz. Danny Boyle felt that she was unique among her peers and the combination of her friendly sense of humour and natural manner had instantly appealed to him. 'As soon as she walked in the room, I knew that she was right,' he declared.

Diaz, who familiarised herself with McGregor's work before starting on the movie, later revealed that she had no particular expectations of her co-star. When McGregor learned who his leading lady was to be, he was full of doubts: he had only seen her in the wacky comedy *The Mask* – a film he hates. But, more than that, he was concerned that a Hollywood babe would be synonymous with prima-donna antics. He envisaged a temperamental starlet turning up with a small army for an entourage, demanding three trailers and 'being difficult' – a prospect that would have driven him mad. His fears, however, proved unfounded. He had been swiftly assured that Cameron Diaz was far from difficult and he discovered this for himself when they met for the first time on the film set. 'You worry about famous American actresses being so up their arse,' he said, 'but she's a cracker. No pretence and no hassle at all.'

By contrast, the plot of *A Life Less Ordinary* was entirely sustained by pretence. It tells the story of a bored and beautiful heiress and a young working-class guy who dreams of being a bestselling novelist whilst he is employed as a lowly janitor in the pay of Celine's ruthless businessman father (Ian Holm). This diametrically different pair, at the opposite ends of the social spectrum, are brought together by chance when Robert, newly sacked from his job, storms in a fit of untypical rage into the office to confront his powerful boss. In the resulting melee which verged on slapstick, he finds himself seizing a gun from one of the security guards and abducting Celine, with more than a little help from her. The mayhem that ensues as he takes to the open road with his prisoner is further complicated by the introduction into the story of two angels. They have been sent to earth to make the unlikely couple fall in love – a task which stretches the angels' ingenuity.

Holly Hunter and Delroy Lindo would turn in suitably manic performances as the angels, and Ian Holm, in his few scenes, conveys a believable cold ruthlessness. But the success or failure of the film would ultimately rest with the two central performances and that in itself depended on the screen chemistry between McGregor and Diaz.

Reviewers would later disagree as to whether such a chemistry existed; the actors themselves maintain that it did. Both of them state firmly that they had a ball making the film and that this was self-evident in their screen scenes together. Cameron Diaz later remarked, 'In the film I fall in love with Ewan's character and you can see how any girl could fall for him in real life too. He has sex appeal and is an amazing guy.'

McGregor revealed, 'She's a special girl. You can see in some of the scenes we're genuinely having a laugh with each other and that makes it so much warmer. It heightens all the romance and all the fun scenes. There are real twinkles in our eyes.'

They also found that they had many things in common. Firstly, although both were considered the new 'hot shots on the block', neither had any truck with behaving in a starry fashion. Theirs was a gruelling schedule, with between twelve and sixteen-hour days, and during those long spells when they awaited the call back on set they watched countless videos of old movies together. Diaz, like McGregor, came from a solid family background and was close to her parents. The two actors also shared a wicked sense of humour, verging on the scatological; their adjoining trailers, partitioned by only a wafer-thin division, meant that each heard the other visiting the bathroom. They were later said to have shared many a joke through this wall whilst sitting on their respective toilets. Cameron Diaz's sense of adventure also greatly appealed to the bold McGregor; whereas his real passion was for motorbikes, he also liked driving cars, and so did Diaz. In fact, the spark between the two young actors, whilst shooting and later during the PR round of interviews, was such that the almost obligatory rumours quickly began circulating. But life was not imitating art.

Although the central characters in *A Life Less Ordinary* eventually do fall in love and marry, apart from a handful of screen kisses and one moment when Diaz slinks suggestively and half-dressed away from a dazed McGregor sprawled in his crumpled bed, there was no actual sex scene in this romance: something about which, despite McGregor's past nonchalance, he seemed to be relieved. It would later transpire that his wife Eve had been unhappy about the nude sex scene he had enacted with Kelly Macdonald in *Trainspotting* – an attitude that McGregor found no difficulty in understanding. 'It can cause emotional damage,' he once stated, 'to watch your loved one being intimate with someone else, even if it is part of the job.'

It often also goes with the territory, when two attractive stars team up, for speculation to begin as to whether their on-screen romance was being mirrored in an off-screen affair. But this time such rumours would find no basis, especially when it emerged that not only was Cameron Diaz involved with actor Matt Dillon – he was frequently around the set – but that McGregor had taken his wife and child with him to Utah. All too aware that showbusiness is a graveyard for marriage, he was determined not to risk his own swelling the divorce statistics. To this end he had begun having a special clause written into his contracts: whenever his work took him away from home for any length of time, his wife and child were to accompany him on location. 'I am in a position to insist that they come, and if anyone doesn't like that, then I won't make the film,' he declares. Eve and Clara, therefore, had accompanied him to the States and rented a house near to Salt Lake City for the duration of his stay.

None of this meant, however, that the irrepressible McGregor was not fully aware that the chance to smooch with the blonde, blue-eyed, slender screen goddess Cameron Diaz was the fetish of many a young man, including his own (happily married) brother. He laughingly described his friends' response when he landed the chance to co-star with Diaz: 'I've never been sworn at so much! They were like – "Fuck you, bastard!" ' And of his brother Colin's reaction, McGregor gleefully reported, 'Things like that really piss him off. He's fucking gutted and I love it!' He added, 'I had to get her to sign a picture for him which he has above his bed.'

For McGregor there were other attractions in playing this latest part, beyond working with his three film-making friends. 'I loved the idea of the romantic comedy. I tend to be cast as cynical characters, but in *A Life Less Ordinary* I play a sweet, innocent guy. There's more humour in this than anything I've previously done.' Despite the hard-edged characters he habitually portrays he admits that in real life he can be romantic to the point of being sentimental and so he welcomed the opportunity, in this film, to explore the more tender side of life. 'I made an effort to be unashamed about it,' he later stated, 'because we're surrounded by so much cynicism these days that it's difficult to pull it off. We all do it, but nobody wants to watch it any more, which I think is a bit of a shame.'

As Robert, he portrays a Scot working in the States, which removed the task of having to adopt an American accent for the second time. Fortunately, unlike some Scottish dialects which can prove pretty impenetrable to anyone outside Scotland, McGregor's natural accent has a clarity that renders it easily comprehensible. But he has spoken publicly about a pitfall he encounters from time to time, 'If I'm putting on an accent and I have to be angry in a scene, my Scottish accent will always slip through a bit, because we're very angry people.' Whilst admitting that he can tire of using his 'own' voice McGregor said, of *A Life Less Ordinary*, 'It's just easier working with the team that way. They're used to me speaking with a Scottish accent.' But he also added that, whenever he did use his own voice in a film, he felt exposed.

Trust, however, so vital to an actor, was never in short supply in this film. Part of a director's lot is to be ruthless, which can, on occasion, leave actors feeling callously humiliated. But, said McGregor, 'Danny never lets me down. I'd do anything for him – paint my arse blue and run round naked in Central Park if he wanted me to.' Which just about summed up McGregor's whole attitude to this film and the hundred per cent effort he gave for Boyle. 'He drains your creative juices,' he went on, 'and makes you work. But you want to push everything out for him anyway.' Such was his passion to please, he said, 'It could have been our first movie together.'

Making *A Life Less Ordinary*, however, did prove to be arduous in some respects. McGregor later referred to his stay in Utah as 'a whole other experience'. In fact, he had been appalled on arrival to discover that it was not possible to readily obtain an alcoholic drink; Utah was a dry state and to buy alcohol there one required a licence, which he did not have. This meant that in order to seek out a beer after work ended for the day, the cast and crew had to motor miles in search of a public house. They eventually landed lucky by discovering Spankys, a bar, not for the faint-hearted, in Salt Lake City. Spankys was frequented by bikers, but far from being intimidated by the butch clientele, McGregor was completely at home in the place. He loved it so much that, as Cameron Diaz later revealed, night after night so reluctant was he to leave that he had to be literally dragged out. And McGregor would fondly recall, 'One night I beat the fucking shit out of Danny Boyle on the pool table. The next day he said that he couldn't believe it because I was so drunk I could hardly speak and yet I was hammering the balls in.'

Certainly McGregor found the atmosphere of the deeply religious Mormon community personally oppressive. He had been pre-warned that Utah was a 'dodgy state'. 'And it really is,' he would later conclude, adding that it was inhabited by 'the weirdest fucking people I've ever met'. He felt that he had detected a peculiar reaction to the sight of him walking about with his baby daughter – he maintained that they hated it because, in the first place, a child denoted that he had had some fun in his world, and also that they disapproved of his scruffy dress style. He also called Salt Lake City a beautiful but strange place. 'The whole town is built in this bowl where you are absolutely safe from any normal life. It is built next to this huge, stagnant and stinking lake. I was pleased to get away from it,' he said as the whole cast and crew vacated Utah for one last week of filming in Los Angeles.

When the filming wrapped Danny Boyle's enthusiasm about McGregor led him to claim that he was Daniel Day-Lewis and Gary Oldman rolled into one. Boyle did have a valid point when he talked of the actor's similarity to Hollywood star Tom Hanks: both men have the ability to portray the inoffensive guy-next-door. 'He has got that ordinariness,' said the director. 'He doesn't try to represent himself without spots.'

It was true that McGregor's acting style was, more and more, becoming distinguished by an easy instinctiveness. 'I just see what happens at the time on the set,' he said, unwilling as always to analyse himself too deeply. But what was also plain was that time and again, in different ways, he also allowed his personal blend of magnetism to waft through his performances. Screen charisma is a crucial weapon in the armoury of most of today's biggest box-office draws, and in *A Life Less Ordinary*, McGregor had unquestionably delivered.

McGregor believes that US audiences are more intrigued by British actors because they appear more vulnerable than their American macho counterparts. So he depicted Robert as hapless but not helpless, with an ineptitude that seemed entirely realistic and excusable; moreover, he made the audience want to protect him.

At the outset of the project, writer John Hodge had said, 'After the first two, which are both quite dark and morbid films, we wanted to do something that was more optimistic and wasn't afraid to show some honest sentiment.' And *A Life Less Ordinary* was, in that sense, a brave departure for the *Shallow Grave/Trainspotting* celebrated team. The film, as McGregor vehemently insists, was like its predecessors not mainstream. Not as such, anyway. But it was reminiscent of a certain genre of movie: the romantic fantasy. The problem lay in the attempt to update this genre.

Old Hollywood had had these fantasies, which often featured bungling celestial bodies who intervened to bring about a happy ending, down to a fine art. But then, they were making films for a far less cynical audience: recreating the formula for the 1990s was full of pitfalls. It didn't help that the team behind *A Life Less Ordinary* had so far excelled only in the field of darkness and death, grit and greed. It was very hard for example, to reconcile the ultimate sweet intentions of the angels with the particularly nasty violence they inflicted on the couple.

The use of guns had been a conscious decision on the film-makers' part. Boyle declared that drama down the years traditionally provided an essential vehicle for such weaponry. 'You go to the cinema to see things played out that will never play any part in your life,' he said. John Hodge called it a cinematic convention and producer Andrew Macdonald was defensive. 'Our violence is nothing.' Not when compared with many other films. But *A Life Less Ordinary* wasn't supposed to be that sort of movie.

The use of guns certainly bothered McGregor during his preparation period, when he made visits to a gun range to learn to shoot. In a land overrun with firearms, it was his first time handling a hand gun – in this case a snub-nose .45. Some claim that guns produce an empowering sensation, but McGregor was not turned on, and he felt even more concerned when he was taken into one of America's many vast gun shops. What amazed McGregor most was to discover that it was as impersonal and everyday as a supermarket. Later he did not mince his words. 'It was fuckin' terrifying. Just full of things to kill people.'

After its August premiere at the Edinburgh Film Festival, *A Life Less Ordinary* was released simultaneously in Britain and in the States on 24 October 1997. Once again in the period surrounding the film's release, its makers and stars were out in force on the promotion circuit, with Cameron Diaz often joining McGregor as a kind of lively double act – a two-for-one bonus for journalists eager to get the lowdown on just how close the actors had become during the film.

McGregor could not resist the opportunity to tease. On one occasion in New York, during a solo interview, he was confronted by a reporter whom he found particularly pushy. By this time, McGregor was becoming ever more adept at handling the Press and he was well aware that this guy was trying to trawl for dirt on Cameron Diaz, waiting for that head-line-grabbing one-liner. Recounting this experience, McGregor told of how he kept the journalist at bay with pleasant but innocuous remarks about the actress – until the man's tape ran out. Then, in a split-second and completely straight-faced, out of the blue he said, 'And that was when I fucked her.' Laughing at the memory of how the stunned journalist had been taken in, McGregor went on, 'He scrambled to put his tape back on, but he'd missed it.'

Devilment aside, it was in the main the reviewers who had the last laugh. Andrew Macdonald had predicted that the *Trainspotting* team was probably due for a kicking; prior to the first preview screening of *A Life Less Ordinary* it struck some critics that the producer appeared to be dampening the assembled audience's expectations of what they were about to see. McGregor too seemed to be in a similar downbeat frame of mind. 'People expect it to be what it's not,' he warned. 'I think it's risky because it's an American romantic comedy.'

The reviews, though mixed, clearly weighed down on the side of it being a disappointment. The attack was two-pronged. One went for the fabled film-maker trio: 'An implausible shambles by the *Trainspotting* team.' declared the *Daily Mail*, while *The Guardian* described them as 'not as clever or dark as they think they are'. Others joined in, declaring that they had crashed to earth with an almighty thud, with one critic observing that if Boyle's aim had been to beat the Yanks at their own game on their own turf, then the director 'has fallen flat on his face'. Some pinpointed what they felt were substantial conceptual flaws in the film; the movie was also dubbed 'a puddle of self-consciousness'. 'With such a splendid title and potentially interesting ingredients, why does it so horribly misfire and fall to pieces?' asked the *Sunday Times*.

The other prong of attack focused on the stars themselves and the film's reliance on their personal chemistry. Many critics zeroed in on what they perceived as the lack of screen connection between the two, pointing out that because Diaz was *so* glamorous and McGregor *so* ordinary their relationship simply wasn't plausible. Against her ruthless sophistication, McGregor's shaggy mop top, baggy shirt and pale face had saddled him with the disadvantage of looking, one reviewer complained, 'less like Diaz's lover and more like her spotty younger brother'. And while the super svelte actress fairly radiated poise and star quality McGregor, he continued, seemed merely to absorb it.

In their defence, the *Trainspotting* team tried again to convey their collective philosophy; that they had no interest in standing still. 'You've got to try and change,' they stressed. Where the trio would professionally go next lay open to speculation, as did whether the partnership would remain intact. John Hodge had not been present on location for *A Life Less Ordinary*; he had remained in Britain to complete a contract as a senior registrar at a London hospital. 'I miss working as a doctor. I don't want to write screenplays for the rest of my life. I would get bored of the film industry even if I'm successful.' There was also, naturally, much talk centred around the fact that this was McGregor's third and perhaps final collaboration with the three. Andrew Macdonald announced that the actor was, 'part of our core team. It's four of us now'. To which one critic responded by urging that McGregor would be wise at this juncture to 'quit his current role as a young mascot for the *Trainspotting* gang'.

McGregor, of all people, was unlikely to be influenced by such advice, however. 'I would turn down any of these bloomin' multi-million pound things if it meant conflicting with something he [Danny Boyle] wanted me to do.' He also stated, 'Whether I'll play the lead in their movies all the time is up to them. Their loyalty to me is 100 per cent, but if I wasn't right for the character then, of course, I'd respect their decision.'

Amidst the flak over *A Life Less Ordinary*, McGregor was gratified when his performance was described, by some, as his best comic turn to date. 'I was more aware of being funny,' he says, 'but that isn't done by trying to play the comedy. You're still playing the character in a real situation.' Some other critics pointed out that McGregor's vibrant personality and inherent *niceness* had been allowed a welcome chance to shine through for the first time in his career to date. And that was considered to be no bad thing.

Precisely because the haunted face *Trainspotting*'s Mark Renton was so burned into the public's collective consciousness, it would soon be deemed advantageous for McGregor to be seen in his new role as a boy-next-door. For he would be required to shake the remaining dust of the amoral junkie association from his shoes in order to take on the mantle of every schoolboy and girl's space hero in *Star Wars*. This gigantic leap in his career had yet to happen, but was not that far away when, as he entered 1997, the new year brought with it the dawn of a new era in his professional world.

CHAPTER 9

All That Glitters

DESPITE THE CRITICISM levelled at *A Life Less Ordinary* the film attracted, at least for McGregor, yet more awards to add to the slew of accolades he was fast acquiring. For the third consecutive time he would walk off with the Best British Actor trophy in the 1997 *Empire* Movie Awards, beating off competition from Ralph Fiennes for *The English Patient*, Robert Carlyle for *The Full Monty* and Ray Winstone in *Nil By Mouth*. McGregor had attended the glitzy event, held at London's Park Lane Hotel, on the understanding that he was there to present the Best Actress award and was taken by surprise when he won an award of his own. 'This is lovely – and ridiculous', he said, going on to extol the successful year the British Film Industry as a whole had enjoyed. He ended with a war cry, 'Let's carry on!' As a one-man ambassador for the business he certainly carried on; he would also – in addition to having mopped up the Best British Actor prize for *Trainspotting* from the London Film Critics' Circle – be named the Variety Club of Great Britain's Best Film Actor for his part in *Trainspotting*.

His enhanced superstar profile was further reflected by his high positioning in various popularity polls, come spring 1997. Readers of *Cosmopolitan* magazine voted him third in the 'Ten Sexiest Men on Earth' stakes, behind American heart-throbs George Clooney and Keanu Reeves. And he ranked top of a separate poll charting the 'Men Most Women Would Like to Marry', beating into second and third place respectively, Colin Firth – a hot contender following his sizzling portrayal of Mr Darcy in a BBC TV adaptation of Jane Austen's *Pride and Prejudice* – and, again, George Clooney, from the US hit TV medical drama *ER*.

It was to be *ER* that would produce for McGregor arguably his highest honour yet, when he received a much-coveted Emmy nomination – America's television equivalent of Oscar nominations – in the Outstanding Guest Appearance in a Drama Series category for his role in the episode entitled *The Long Way Around*. McGregor was already a confirmed fan of the Chicago-based hospital drama when he was given a chance to take part in one of the shows whilst he was in the States filming *A Life Less Ordinary*. Said McGregor, 'I was chatting with my agent in Los Angeles about the programme and he said he represented some of *ER*'s cast. A couple of days later they came back and said, "Do you want to be in one?" And I said yes. I did it because I thought it would be a laugh to see myself in one of the episodes with people I'm used to watching in it. And it was.'

In *The Long Way Around*, directed by Christopher Chulack, he plays a character called Duncan Stewart – once again a Scot abroad, this time a redundant Glaswegian shipyard worker who has come to visit his American cousin. Together they attempt to rob a convenience store at gunpoint. The robbery goes wrong, however, and, quickly out of his depth in this situation, he takes hostages, including one of *ER*'s main stars Nurse Carol Hathaway, played by Julianna Margulies. It becomes Nurse Hathaway's task to gain the trust of the two desperate men so that they will allow her to tend to wounded staff and customers.

'I play a Scottish maniac,' he said of hot-headed Duncan Stewart, describing his role in what many considered to be a particularly riveting episode of *ER*. He is eventually gunned down and is already dead on arrival at the hospital, a bloodstained corpse in the stark operating room in the final reel. The claustrophobic setting of the besieged grocery store added to the dramatic tension, which McGregor heightened by channelling all his energies into a skilfully edgy performance as a frantic gunman. 'Corny but captivating,' cried one critic, 'A truly compelling episode,' vouched another when *The Long Way Around* was shown on British screens on Channel 4 on Sunday 13 April 1997.

The undoubted centre of attention on the *ER* set is the dark-eyed handsome Dr Doug Ross, portrayed by George Clooney, one of America's most loved megastars. As the latest actor to play the big-screen *Batman*, Clooney's fame is such that normal privacy is simply not possible.

Reputedly, he has to endure Press helicopters frequently circling above his house in an endless search for photographs and/or a story. Still, this invasive pressure seems not to have dented his easy-going attitude towards the show's other cast members and guest stars – as McGregor discovered. 'George Clooney really is a very nice guy,' he said afterwards. 'He's very fatherly on set and looks after everyone.' McGregor was also pleased to have had the opportunity of adding Julianna Margulies to the lengthening list of his attractive leading ladies. 'She's beautiful, isn't she?' he said.

Ever eager to broaden his experience, McGregor approached this one-off television opportunity conscientiously. Presumably in an effort to make their latest guest star feel at home, the writer of this particular episode, Lydia Woodward, injected a lot of references to Scotland into the script, only to bow to McGregor's finer feelings. 'We took a few out,' he revealed, 'because I thought there were too many.' And the experience opened his eyes in other ways. *ER*'s executive producer, John Wells, admits that their aim, right from the start, has always been to hook viewers and force them to tune in for each of the twenty-three episodes of every series: to achieve that, the show had to be extremely fast-paced. 'If we slow down for a few seconds,' he explains, 'the audience can go to one of a hundred other channels.'

McGregor's delight at his involvement with *ER* suffered a dent, however, when it transpired that one airline official astonishingly seemed to confuse Ewan's most famous film character with the real-life actor – as McGregor himself later revealed. 'I got fucking stripsearched at Chicago airport. My visa had Warner Brothers on it and some customs guy asked me about my movies and I said the only ones known in America were *Shallow Grave* and *Trainspotting*. And he said, "*Trainspotting!*" and writes something on my form and when I get to the red and green bit they searched me everywhere . . . even up the arse! Fucking stupid bastard!'

Whilst the vast Warner Brothers studio lot in Los Angeles is the main production centre of the series hailed as the most successful American drama of the decade, filming does also take place in Chicago. As the main guest star McGregor had, towards the end of *A Life Less Ordinary*, joined Clooney, Margulies and other regulars, including Anthony Edwards, to shoot the episode on its regular punishing schedule of just eight thirteen-hour working days. In the circumstances it was hardly a surprise when

McGregor declared, 'It was a much faster shoot than anything I've ever been used to.'

Appearing in this one-hour slot on prime-time television in both America and Britain would also broaden his exposure. Where *ER* chalks up impressive Channel 4 audiences of around five million in the UK, it occupies one of America's top three TV slots; in addition the series is exported to over seventy other countries around the globe. McGregor insists, 'I didn't do *ER* to help me break into the States.' But it would none the less have done his already high profile the power of good; moreover, he would be keeping good company in appearing as a guest star in this weekly drama. In the previous series film director Quentin Tarantino both directed and appeared in one show, and director Joel Schumacher was set to follow. There was only one casualty of this one-off appearance, as McGregor explains. 'I haven't watched the programme since, because now I know the set and stuff, the magic has sort of gone.'

It was to bring a little magic to ordinary lives that McGregor was prepared to interrupt a precious family break in February 1997 to visit his old school in Crieff. His one-day visit to Morrison's Academy had originally been planned for the end of January, but had had to be rescheduled when he was recalled to the *ER* set for a few extra minutes' filming. He explains, 'They had to shoot another scene when they discovered they were going to be a bit short for the episode.' It was on 7 February, therefore, that he created a local storm of excitement by returning to his old stomping ground.

It was a strange experience for him, especially since, by the very nature of an old boy's return to school as a celebrity, such occasions are usually meant to be a shining example of what that person's years at that establishment enabled him to achieve. In McGregor's case, as he had often remarked in the intervening ten years, he had not exactly hated school, but he had not felt that it provided, at any rate for him, what he wanted from life. Still, as an ex-pupil turned world-famous star, he was prepared to enter into the spirit of things. McGregor would state whilst there, 'I always knew what I wanted to do. If you're passionate and set on something, you'll get there.' He added, 'I got a lot out of my days here.'

Whatever he said, he was there in the flesh – that was all that was needed for the delighted pupils clamouring desperately to see him. The media, too, flocked to capture the event, keen not to miss any happening involving the actor currently being tipped as hot favourite to become Hollywood's next superstar. Even if it only meant taking a drama master-class with the cast of the Crieff school's forthcoming amateur production of *Tom Sawyer*.

As is the case for anyone who has outgrown their school years, return-ing to the focus of so many memories is to find that it no longer seems such a daunting place. The building itself even seemed smaller to McGregor; it certainly reverberated with a more relaxed atmosphere than he remembered, although he still felt most uncomfortable during his first task: appearing alongside the Rector Gareth Edwards, at assembly, and being introduced to the whole school.

Characteristically he handled the entire visit with smiling good humour. During the course of the day he gave talks about acting; shed light on the behind-the-scenes life; and got physical with a string of stu-dents who quickly fell into line to trade punches with him after he had taken them through the various steps of choreographing a convincing screen fight. Apart from the drama workshop, he met with senior sixth-form pupils to discuss the current state of the British film industry. And he thrilled the delirious teenage girls who braved the icy conditions and blustering snow to mob him in the school grounds, where he patiently signed autographs on any and all of the assorted items pressed feverishly into his hands before giving a press conference, at which he faced ques-tions from four television crews, eight national newspaper journalists and a national radio reporter

One of McGregor's last tasks at Morrison's was providing an in-depth interview for the Academy's forthcoming school yearbook. Then, having given the battery of photographers endless photo opportunities, it was over and he was gone. He had lit up the lives of the children in Crieff for a day – but now he had his own youngster to think of.

While he was finishing filming his appearance in *ER*, a real-life domestic medical drama was unfolding at home. Because his absence would be brief his wife and daughter had remained in London and during this time Clara had fallen ill. She developed a high temperature; in addition the baby's limbs had become frighteningly lethargic and Eve wasted no time in rushing her to the Chelsea and Westminster Hospital, by which time the little girl was deeply unconscious. To Eve's horror the doctors diagnosed meningitis.

Ewan received the nightmare news by telephone in Los Angeles and caught the first flight home. He later described the sight that greeted his frantic arrival at his daughter's bedside. 'By the time I got there, all I saw was this little grey baby with tubes up her nose, wired to a heart machine.' He added, 'Eve was kicking herself with guilt over the whole thing, although she did brilliantly. She got her in there, after all. If it had been twenty-four hours later, it would have been too late.'

During the two and a half weeks that Clara remained in hospital, Ewan admitted that he went slightly mad with sheer exhaustion and stress. She made a complete recovery – but not before frightening her parents witless. Talking of this trying time McGregor would reveal that the biggest and best thing about 1997 was the survival of his little girl. 'It's the scariest thing that has ever happened – and the happiest,' he told reporters.

That was afterwards. Understandably, at the time of the scare, fear for his child's health considerably shortened his fuse when journalists, on the scent of the drama, tracked him down. He found it particularly offensive when one *News Of The World* hack buttonholed him on his doorstep. McGregor recalled the moment, claiming that he had been able to tell from some distance away that the man was from this particular tabloid newspaper. 'He wanted to know about my daughter being ill and I just about took his head off.' McGregor found himself especially annoyed at the man using Clara's christian name. 'I could have fucking swung for the cunt,' he angrily declared, although he did not.

This level of protectiveness signposted his continuing devotion to his family. He finds no conflict, no need for bridges, between his professional and private lives. Unlike some actors he does not feel the strain of living in two worlds connected by a sometimes confusing revolving door. 'I don't go to work and then turn into someone else when I return home. I am the same person. My family and my career *are* my life,' he states. 'They are not separate.' When McGregor had been required to shed weight fast for *Trainspotting*, Eve had been instrumental in organising for him a regime of diet and exercise: just one way in which she encourages and supports him. And the support goes both ways. On *A Life Less Ordinary* Eve was assistant to the art director. She had also turned to writing, and was adapting a

In 1998 Ewan took on a £250 a week theatre role in
Little Malcolm and His Struggle Against the Eunuchs. He worked
with his uncle, Denis Lawson, who directed.

Spanish novel into English. Thus the McGregor special arrangement – wherever he goes filming, his family goes too – would not prove to be an impediment to his wife's own plans. 'If she's writing, she can write any-where we are in the world,' says McGregor. 'She's not about to give up on herself. I wouldn't want her to anyway.'

He also maintains, along the way, a lively social life. His married state doesn't necessitate for him a quiet housebound existence. 'I like going out and Eve likes staying home,' he reveals. 'So there's some balance there, plus a lot of arguments. French women can be difficult – but I like difficult women,' he challenges, with a twinkle in his eyes. The old adage about fame and youth being a lethal combination seems to have found an exception in Ewan McGregor. 'I love a pint. I love loads of them,' he has regularly admitted, adding that as yet he has never been found in the gutter. But he has no destructive streak and is never tempted off the straight and narrow by any of the beautiful women he encounters. 'Eve never has to worry about me straying,' he has declared. 'She knows I'd never do that.' He adds, for good measure, 'She knows I'm a scallywag, but I'm not one who's gonna fuck around with her.'

It was when returning home one night after an evening out with his wife that McGregor was confronted by an odd incident: one that stuck out in his mind and which connected in a roundabout manner with a famous casualty of an excessive lifestyle. In April 1994 Kurt Cobain, lead singer with the rock group Nirvana, having survived a drugs overdose the pre-vious month, committed suicide with a shotgun. A few years on, the McGregors were walking home through London's Notting Hill Gate when they were approached by another young couple, apparently seeking directions. Says McGregor, 'They were very obviously E'd out of their nuts and they wanted to know where the park was.' As he gave directions the youth, no longer listening, loomed close to McGregor's face, staring wildly. The boy then gasped, 'You're Kurt Cobain!'

To which McGregor, in quickfire fashion, responded, 'Just don't fuckin' tell anyone! OK?'

By mid-March 1997 the three-month break he had insisted on taking with his family after the completion of filming *A Life Less Ordinary* was almost at an end and the time to start work on a new project was drawing near. But before that he had a return visit to make to Los Angeles, this time for pleasure; he and Eve would be attending the annual Oscar ceremony. John Hodge had been nominated for the 1996 Best Adapted Screenplay award for *Trainspotting* and he wanted to be there to see if his friend would win the prestigious gold-plated statuette.

Held each year at the Shrine Auditorium in South Central LA the Academy Awards ceremony, which is watched by over three billion people worldwide, has been variously described as 'the Superbowl for the film industry' and 'the biggest shop window in the world'. It is also the biggest prize in the world of entertainment, with a hugely lucrative spin-off, as Quentin Tarantino explains. 'If you get even a nomination your movie gets a virtual re-release and can make more than double what it's already made.'

To get an Oscar nomination is also to be viewed not so much as a personal but as a major marketing opportunity. Overnight Hollywood becomes the land of perks and freebies for nominees, with companies desperate to persuade you to endorse their product. Life degenerates into a blur of photo opportunities and interviews; having become public property, the media demands to know all there is to know about you. It was for these reasons that John Hodge stayed in London in the chaotic run-up to Oscar night on 24 March, not even attending a lavish nominees' dinner at the Beverly Hills Hotel and shunning the chance to mingle with Hollywood's hierarchy.

McGregor was less reticent. For him Oscar time meant yet another eye-opening experience, even though he retains his strongly-hold opinions about refusing to be swept up into the Hollywood vortex. 'Even that night I thought: it'd be great to win one but to be in and still on the outside.'

Still, it was hard not to find the sheer extravagance of the occasion impressive. 'It was like Christmas, Glasgow on Hogmanay – bigger than that.' He grabbed the chance to drive around in a flashy rented 1966 Buick Skylark Convertible – 'sex on wheels' he called it. The glitzy parties all melted one into another, resulting in a memorable time made even more special by Hodge's triumph – especially so in the light of the extremely stiff competition he had been up against, including the hotly-tipped Anthony Minghella for *The English Patient* and the Pulitzer Prize-winning playwright Arthur Miller for *The Crucible*. After all the hype was over, the fizz soon fell flat on the champagne but when McGregor left Los Angeles he took something of the glamour and artifice of showbiz with him. For within days he was due on the set of his latest film, in which he was to portray a wasted Seventies rock star.

McGregor had not even started school when glam rock filled the gap in the British music scene after the heady inspirational Sixties had fragmented and before the dark, aggressive punk rock rage arrived in the mid-Seventies. The tag of 'glam rock' was a phrase coined by the journalists: according to Gary Glitter – for years widely regarded as the outrageous king of this flamboyant trend – it was more accurate to think of it as 'theatrical' rock.

Its exponents included, among others, the late Marc Bolan of T-Rex, bands such as Sweet and Slade and, of course, David Bowie's alter ego Ziggy Stardust with his bright orange hair, heavy make-up, skimpy kimono and knee-high boots. The superficial accent was on dressing up and having fun, but this was plastered over the cracks of a colourful culture soaked for some in psychedelic substance abuse and one that was intent on blurring sexual distinctions. It was in these wildly androgynous days that the movie *Velvet Goldmine* was to be set. As McGregor arrived back in Britain he was ready and eager to roll back time and taste to a world suffused with satin, flares, tank tops and chunky platform shoes.

The film, set and shot in and around London, unfolds in flashback as an investigative reporter sets out to unravel the mystery of what had happened to fictitious decadent rock star Brian Slade. Slade had apparently faked his own on-stage murder and mysteriously vanished ten years previously at the peak of his popularity. Slade was to be played by twenty-year-old Irish actor Jonathan Rhys Meyers in his first big screen lead; McGregor's was a major supporting role as Curt Wild, a crazed rock idol, undoubtedly based on drummer/vocalist Iggy Pop. As McGregor looked ahead to his forthcoming film during the press conference at Morrison's Academy he was playing his cards close to his chest. 'My character is a loose amalgam of a couple of people. Better not say any more in case I get sued,' he joked. 'But it's a great story.'

To help illuminate the lurid tale, casting director Susie Figgis had brought on board a wide variety of talents. Christian Bale, who ten years earlier, as a child newcomer had starred in the Steven Spielberg-directed acclaimed movie *Empire of the Sun*, would handle the third central male character, journalist Arthur Stuart. There was stand-up comedian Eddie Izzard as rock star manager Jerry Devine. And Emily Woof, playing Shannon, joined actress Toni Collette as Mandy Slade – who, describing herself as 'fixated' by the best script she had ever read, revealed her initial anxieties about taking on the role of Mandy, 'I didn't think I was right for the part.' Critical praise for her performance would prove her wrong about that.

This vibrant ensemble lay in the hands of the American film director Todd Haynes, winner of the 1987 Golden Gate Award for *Superstar: The Karen Carpenter Story*. Alongside him he had producer Christine Vachon, his long-standing collaborator. Haynes was always determined to cast McGregor in *Velvet Goldmine*. 'When I first started thinking about my movie, he was the one actor I knew I wanted to use from the start. There's no one else with Ewan's sort of intensity around. Ewan has an incredible, raw power on-screen that I don't think you find among American actors of his generation.'

The executive producer and musical supervisor on the project was Michael Stipe, singer/songwriter with the American rock band REM, who had recently confirmed his interest in the film world by forming the Single Cell Pictures film production company, with New Line Cinema, in September 1994. Stipe was charged with the responsibility of overseeing the movie's soundtrack. With this in mind he roped in several real-life performers to play pop stars – and hopefully make the film more appealing to a youth audience. So guitarist Donna Matthews from the group Elastica portrays a leather-clad lady rocker; and Flaming Creatures, a fictitious group in the film, partly comprises members of the androgynous band Placebo. Filming would take place at Brixton Academy in South London before moving to Bray Studios near Slough; the two-month shooting schedule would stretch into late May. As always, McGregor was revving up to get stuck in.

Like Toni Collette, McGregor had been very excited by the lively script and was relishing the prospect of playing the part of the dangerously sexy wild man of rock. Then he received a phone call from his agent – Lindy King – that would temporarily, but effectively, stop him in his high-heeled tracks. She was calling to tell him that he had landed a role that was an actor's dream – of Obi-Wan Kenobi in George Lucas's forthcoming *Star Wars* prequel movie. But – and this was the killer – he was under strict orders not to tell a soul.

The task of keeping such thrilling news to himself almost defeated him but with supreme willpower he managed to contain his joy, although he made a curious sight for some as he walked about the *Velvet Goldmine* set biting down hard on a clenched fist. 'God knows what everyone thought I was so happy about,' he later ventured. It was inevitable that such pent-up delirium would burst out at some point, but right then he had a job to do, and he focused all his attention on being Curt Wild.

The movie title, *Velvet Goldmine*, was the name of a David Bowie song which had appeared on a three-track re-issue of *Space Oddity*, which had topped the UK charts in November 1975. But the film's producers had run into an obstacle during pre-production when they sought permission from Bowie to use six of his songs, mostly from the 1972 hit album *The Rise And Fall Of Ziggy Stardust And The Spiders From Mars*.

The film's gender-bending lead character Brian Slade was thought by some to have been partly inspired by David Bowie in his bisexual Seventies' incarnation. And any hint of a perceived character association constituted a sticking point. New York-based Henry Wrenn Melek supervises all licensing of Bowie recordings; on receiving the request for permission to use these songs, he had read the film script.

He explained to reporters, 'If one of David's songs was used while something *interesting* was happening on screen, viewers might get the impression that everything they were seeing was factual.' A spokeswoman for the film company had already described the main thrust of *Velvet Goldmine* as dwelling more on the sexual than the drug-taking aspects of the decade. 'It is to do with bisexuality and challenging the sexual conventions of the time,' she stated. The answer to the licensing request from the Bowie camp was an emphatic no. They did make clear, though, that their refusal was for purely commercial reasons: plans, it emerged, were on hand to produce, over the next decade, a complete catalogue of Bowie's work and these specific numbers – some of Bowie's biggest hits – would obviously be included. Wrenn Melek stressed that it was nothing personal. 'It wouldn't matter if Martin Scorsese wanted them. The answer would be no.'

This refusal was initially disappointing to the film-makers. Director Todd Haynes recalls, 'It was crushing at the time but it was a nice opportunity to feature songs that had been forgotten.'

For McGregor the role of the unstable rock diva would add yet another colourful character to his crowded closet of screen personae. There was also no doubt that, in respect of permitting McGregor the chance to portray a rock star, *Velvet Goldmine* was for him, a dream fulfilled. He had always had a passion for singing and when the role of Curt Wild had appeared on his horizon, this time he had had an extra condition of acceptance. 'They offered me the job and there are four or five concert numbers in it. So I said I'd do it, if they let me sing live. It seemed like a great idea at the time. Of course, five minutes before I had to go on, I was a nervous wreck. But it was just brilliant. I was able to be a rock star for a couple of minutes.'

He went on, 'I was trying to get over this Oasis hump thing. Since Oasis came out I've sort of had this desperate desire to be a rock star so I thought if I played one maybe I would get over it.' McGregor admitted, though, that the Seventies might not have been his ideal choice of era into which to plunge. 'I was never really into glam rock. I thought it was a bit silly. I remember *Top Of The Pops* and seeing these guys with weird hair and make-up and thinking, they look a shambles.' He was relieved therefore that his particular character came from the States. 'Because I'm the American guy I'm wearing lots of leathers and hipsters so I got off quite lightly in terms of what some of the other guys had to wear – high camp stuff. I got the kind of grungy look, which is good.' Despite the relative straightness of his image, he still got into the swing of things. 'I loved dressing up. I kept saying, "More eyeliner, more!" I was such a slut.'

As part of his preparation for Curt Wild, he watched videos of inspirational pop performers of the past in order to absorb the flavour of the Seventies. He called Wild 'the American representative', stressing that, while the character definitely wasn't based on one specific person, he 'looked at Iggy Pop stuff and different things from the period just to get some of his moves down. He's an incredible performer. It's been interesting to try and get him.' He went on, 'The voice I tried to get came from listening to Robbie Robertson of The Band. If it ends up like Kurt Cobain, it's completely by chance.' On a first-hand basis, Michael Stipe gave him advice on how to realistically project himself during the gig scenes. Sporting a shoulder-length blond wig styled in a feathercut, tight-fitting clothes and wearing nail varnish and dramatic make-up, which gave his eyes a haunted look, McGregor melted convincingly into character and turned in a penetrating performance which newspaper pundits would be hailing as brilliant long in advance of the movie's release. The film's central themes of drugs, rock and roll and gay sex were nothing new to McGregor; he had handled them all before in various roles. But this hell-raising character gave him more scope than ever to throw caution to the wind – which is precisely what he did at a particular moment during filming in the early hours of one morning.

The suppressed energy he was called upon to display in *Velvet Goldmine* was helped to burn all the brighter by the inner excitement at having bagged the *Star Wars* role. McGregor needed a safety-valve. 'At one point it was four in the morning and we were doing this outdoor concert number and all I had on was a pair of silver leather flared jeans and platform shoes. There were a lot of hippies there and as the glam-rock kicked in they decided that they didn't like what they were hearing. Gradually, through the song, they started booing and telling me to get off. So the director said, "Just flash, give them a moonie." So I did.'

It seems as if he did much more than moon, judging by another version of the same story. 'I was mad when I was doing it,' he remembers. 'I ended up butt-naked in front of 400 extras with my trousers round my ankles, pulling my cock and going, "fuck off!" in a field somewhere south of London.' It would be a scene, that perhaps naturally, became one of the film's most memorable. McGregor maintains, 'That was the heart of my performance. That's what that whole film will always be about for me. The thing is, I enjoy extraordinary situations. I thrive on excess in lots of respects. When I was standing onstage drunk, pulling my penis, bending over and showing them my arsehole – that was an extraordinary situation to find myself in. I got such a buzz out of it. The first time I did a take, I turned around at the end and everyone – the crew, the extras – was literally speechless. It was a great moment. Nobody had anything to say.'

McGregor's antics as Curt Wild in *Velvet Goldmine* and the actor's natural lack of inhibition led him to be asked repeatedly about his now notorious readiness to let it all hang out. His answers were characteristically irrepressible. 'The concert stuff was where I really got my rocks off. I dived into the audience just after pulling everything out again,' he revealed. 'It's great to be getting paid well for doing something that would normally end you up in prison. Women are always being asked to get their kit off. So it's only fair that I get mine out. I'm making a feminist stance by shaking my willy around as much as possible.'

He went on, 'Iggy's got a great love for his penis. I can't say I feel quite the same way. I mean, I don't go around thinking, "Hey, I've got a huge cock. Go on. Show me yours and let's compare sizes." But at the same time, when people ask me if I'd be so keen to flash my willy if it was small, I always think, "Well how the fuck am I supposed to know?" ' (After his nude scenes in *The Pillow Book* the suggestively unsubtle nickname 'Big Mac' had in fact been bestowed upon McGregor.)

In a climate where he was now considered a hot young heart-throb his antics in *Velvet Goldmine* were set to raise temperatures yet again. And, again, he would be taking risks: the sex scenes included bisexual romps. His explicit encounters involved the two characters played by Jonathan Rhys Meyers and Christian Bale. In the case of Meyers, their lurid simulated passion occurs when Curt Wild seduces Brain Slade. It presented McGregor with no problems. 'We're both straight guys, but it was absolutely the same as doing a love scene with an actress.'

He adds, 'It's actually much more exciting being in a sex scene with a man. It's something outside of my normal experience. It's another example of an extreme situation – snogging a man.'

McGregor's professional ease at handling this unique requirement pleased and impressed the director Todd Haynes. 'Ewan was very cool about the sex scenes. I'm not sure an American actor of his age would have been so relaxed. Americans tend to get worried about portraying gay characters – how it will affect their careers. When they do sex scenes, they tend to leap up as soon as you say "cut" and start punching walls to reassert their masculinity. Ewan wasn't like that.'

McGregor's wife Eve Mavrakis had no problems either with the sex scenes in *Velvet Goldmine*, although that had not always been the case. 'Ewan had a sex scene with the actress Kelly Macdonald in *Trainspotting*,' she reveals. Poor Kelly. She's a lovely girl, but at that time I just had a full-blown jealousy thing. If I saw her, my heart started beating fast. I would get out of breath. I could hardly speak to her. It's very weird. But that's the only time.' With *Goldmine* she had an entirely different reaction. 'There he is, having a gay relationship with two different men. I didn't think I could ever relate to that. But actually I found it rather sexy.'

The intensity of concentration required to enact gay or straight sex scenes can leave the actors at the mercy of the director and sometimes, even the film crew. It was while McGregor – in character – was getting all steamed up with Christian Bale in the open air on a King's Cross rooftop that they became the victim of a practical joke. 'I was supposed to be shagging Christian Bale and it went on so long at one point I put my head down beside Christian, away from the camera, and whispered, "I would have come by now, if this was for real!" Then I looked over to see the camera crew packing up. The fuckers didn't say "cut" and we were still giving it our all!'

Jokes aside, by the time filming began drawing to a close McGregor had formed decided views upon some aspects of the experience. It had been months since he had parted company professionally with Danny Boyle, but the memory of their special working relationship had lingered.

When McGregor later spoke of the weeks of filming with Todd Haynes he said, 'It was hard work. I got really pissed off because I generally wanted to rehearse the scenes first. But Todd's approach was, "No. We'll just shoot it." We never rehearsed any scenes. It was almost like shooting by numbers. It was frustrating. I'm slightly spoiled by working with Danny Boyle. This is the trouble now. It gets harder and harder to work with other people because Danny does it the right way, I think.' He went on to insist, 'Todd's done amazing stuff. He's fantastic and I love him to death. It was all to do with time, not his direction. It was having too tight a schedule.'

Everyone connected with the film certainly gave it their all. In McGregor's case sometimes he chose to go the extra mile, judging by the recollections of one of the other actors in the movie, Micko

Westmoreland, who played the character Jack Fairy. He has revealed that, although there was a stunt man on hand, McGregor frequently chose not to make use of the man's services – even when he was required to dive through a wall of flame.

As shooting drew to a close one thing was for certain: McGregor's desire to be a rock star had decidedly diminished. 'I'd be dead. The relentless touring, the buggering about, the fuelled consumption from the endless parties, performing in front of thousands of people. If I did that for more than a week I'd sink into a terrible depression. We have rock stars for a reason. We need them to do it for us.'

As the time approached the following year for *Velvet Goldmine's* general release, it looked like the film-makers had got it right, even although director Todd Haynes revealed that it had been a particularly difficult film to make. 'It was the hardest I've ever done. The script was so ornate, like a jigsaw puzzle, and every piece of that puzzle had to function on its own, which meant that we were very often in one location to shoot an eighth of a page and at another for the next eighth.' He added, 'We ended up having to do the film for a great deal less than the lowest budget we could conceive of.'

The release would prove to be particularly timely. A Seventies revival in Britain – already evident in fashion with the return of platform shoes and flares – was also being reflected in films with the release of movies such as Ang Lee's *The Ice Storm* and Paul Thomas Anderson's *Boogie Nights*. In the summer of 1998 a £3.5 million stage production at the London Palladium of the Seventies monster disco movie *Saturday Night Fever* was taking in ticket sales of more than £350,000 for weeks. Todd Haynes believes, 'The one thing missing from the constant Seventies revivalism is an honest look at how progressive that period was politically and culturally. And to me that's a lot of the excitement in the film. It's not about the sort of naff funny plastic Seventies. It's about something much more important that we really haven't seen the like of since.'

Originally it was intended that *Velvet Goldmine* would come out in Britain in April but editing snags delayed it for a month. Then the summer began to look like an inauspicious time for release – it would clash with the 1998 football World Cup. In the end, September was floated as the likeliest month.

It did, however, premiere at the Cannes Film Festival on Friday 22 May 1998. As the movie industry's movers and shakers swarmed around in the frenzy of a market place where million-dollar deals are won and lost, McGregor's performance and the film *Velvet Goldmine* itself made a dazzling impact.

Of the twenty-three films in competition that year *Velvet Goldmine* would be one of three in the British category for the Festival's top film award, the Palme d'Or, and McGregor's name would be in the frame for the Best Actor award, competing against Johnny Depp, who had partnered Cameron Diaz in *Fear And Loathing In Las Vegas*, and the eventual winner, the relatively unknown Peter Mullan in his first starring role as a recovering alcoholic in Ken Loach's *My Name is Joe*. Unfortunately, although Jonathan Rhys Meyers, Christian Bale, Toni Collette and Eddie Izzard were all personally present in Cannes with Todd Haynes, the ever-busy McGregor was unable to attend due to filming commitments.

Velvet Goldmine's UK premiere took place on Sunday 16 August 1998 when it opened at the Edinburgh Film Festival. This time McGregor was able to attend and he arrived at the Odeon Cinema sporting a designer stubble and dressed in his familiar kilt, this time topped with a thick knitted sweater with a sprig of lucky white heather pinned to his chest. He admits, 'When I saw the movie at the Edinburgh Festival I was truly shocked. I was like, "*Look what I'm doing!*" I was truly exhilarated by watching myself. Does that sound arrogant? It's because I wasn't in control of myself when I was doing it.' His overall verdict on his performance was typically lacking in false modesty 'I think I'd have made a great rock star, just like Elvis.'

The London premiere followed two months later on 19 October at the Curzon Soho cinema, after which a party was held at the Piccadilly club In & Out. McGregor had been photographed grinning broadly on arrival at the cinema, accompanied by his mother, but it appears that he became less enamoured of the occasion later at the premiere bash, where he is reported to have asked co-star Eddie Izzard, on surveying some of the guests present, 'Where did this lot crawl out from? I thought the Seventies was supposed to be the decade that taste forgot?' He let his hair down for a while on the dance floor but eventually slipped off home to Belsize Park.

With the film due to go on general release in Britain on 23 October producer Christine Vachon explained succinctly why there had been a further delay in its release. It seems the makers had been reluctant to clash with *The Truman Story*, the new Jim Carrey movie. 'It [*The Truman Story*] will get all the press. If you open against it, you're screwed.'

Director Haynes still held his aspirations high. 'I would like to see *Velvet Goldmine* compared to *2001* or *Clockwork Orange*. You weren't interested in the plot. The plot was just a way to get you somewhere else.'

Although the soundtrack was applauded, McGregor's American accent was deemed by some critics to be 'wavering' and therefore came in for some stick, and the film itself attracted polarised reviews – *Film Review* decided that it was 'an arresting evocation of a sexually rebellious period, directed with wit, style and imagination' adding that 'the ever reliable McGregor shines'. But *Total Film* magazine roundly denounced it. 'A turd is still a turd no matter how much glitter you sprinkle on it.'

By this stage, even negative reviews couldn't slow McGregor down. The volume of his work was beginning to accumulate as he kept up a breath-less pace that showed no sign of abating. But with *Brassed Off* and *The Pillow Book* now on release in the States to join *Nightwatch* and, later, *A Life Less Ordinary*, in June 1997 he was about to embark on the biggest American movie of his career. For the first of the three planned prequels to the phenomenally successful *Star Wars* trilogy was about to go into production.

'I've really come a long way,' McGregor says, 'but when I heard I'd got *Star Wars* I was *so* excited. I felt just like a big kid.' McGregor's inner knot of intense anticipation was entirely appropriate. He was about to enter new realms – realms which were, in more ways than one, completely out of this world.

CHAPTER 10

Jedi Master

THE FIRST DAY I got dressed properly it was quite a moment for a boy from Scotland to stand there and look in the mirror. "Jedi McGregor".'

McGregor was utterly consumed by the sheer thrill of having the opportunity to go down in film history – as he surely will by being a leading player in a trilogy of mythical movies designed to predate an original three-part huge blockbuster series that began twenty years before and remained – in the case of the first film *Star Wars, A New Hope*, the biggest grossing movie of all time until the arrival in 1997 of the James Cameron-directed film *Titanic*.

Principal photography began on *Star Wars Episode I, The Phantom Menace*, on 3 June 1997. Immediately prior to this date word leaked out that 'the unstoppable Jock', as one newspaper had by now branded McGregor, had secured the lead role. From the moment this became known, much was made of his uncle having been in the original *Star Wars* movie, despite the fact that, as Wedge, Denis Lawson appeared only in the final minutes of a 121-minute movie in a frantic series of cockpit shots as one of several fighter pilots trying to protect the hero Luke Skywalker as he aimed to bomb the Empire's lethal weapon, the Death Star.

McGregor never forgot the excitement he felt seeing Denis on the big screen of his hometown cinema. But it would transpire, years later, that in reality Lawson had not enjoyed filming these scenes. McGregor admits, 'He said it was the worst work he had ever done. Denis said it was absolutely tedious to do.' So tedious, in fact, that Lawson initially queried the wisdom of his nephew taking the lead part in the new film. 'He didn't think I should do it,' says McGregor. 'But I think it would've been very hard to turn down.' McGregor's independent streak allows no one to influence him when he's made up his mind. 'When you're my age and you were out there cheering when the first *Star Wars* came out, what are you going to do when they offer you one of the leads in the new film? Say "No"? No way!' He added, 'It would take a bigger man than me to say no.'

Manoeuvering himself to a position where he even had the chance of landing a role guaranteed to propel any young actor into the showbiz stratosphere had been a slow process. With the whole of Hollywood teeming with actors vying eagerly for the part, the film's casting director Robin Gurland had begun informally chatting to those whom she considered to be likely candidates. Said McGregor, 'As soon as I heard there might be a possibility, it became a kind of mission, because of what *Star Wars* meant to me as a kid.' His meeting with her took place at the start of 1996. Instinctively she believed him to be right for the role, but she continued to explore her options. A year almost to the day later McGregor was recalled for a second and more formal interview, after which he was invited to meet *Star Wars* director and creator George Lucas and the new film's co-producer, Rick McCallum.

Lucas, who in the 1980s had gone on to add the Indiana Jones series of films to his writing and production successes, would be making his first return to the director's chair since the original *Star Wars* movie; he was also funding the production himself. Says McGregor, 'George Lucas was very relaxed, very calm. He didn't make it a big deal. It probably wasn't a big deal to him.' A screen test then followed. 'I did three scenes with Liam Neeson. That was really scary. I was more nervous for that than I have been for a long time,' admits McGregor. Neeson, the Irish star of *Schindler's List* and *Michael Collins*, was being tested for the venerable role of Qui-Gon Jinn, the master Jedi who would train the young Obi-Wan Kenobi. Directors often talk of that special energy which erupts between the commands 'action' and 'cut' and Lucas and McCallum were keen to see if the required screen chemistry would set sparks flying between this would-be master/pupil pairing. McGregor believed, after this adrenalin-driven try-out, that he had done his best. This was borne out by that telephone call from his agent on day one of shooting *Velvet Goldmine*.

The original *Star Wars* movie had adopted the device of engaging the viewer instantly in a struggle that was already long underway. It established that the good guys were the Rebels – the underdog alliance aided by Princess Leia of the Imperial Senate – who were locked in a desperate civil war with the tyrannical Galactic Empire, represented most forcibly by the black-cloaked sinister figure of Darth Vader. Its subtitle of *Episode IV: A New Hope* reinforced the idea that the story had a previous life – Lucas is said to have initially envisaged the saga in nine parts: three parts to pre-date the original trilogy and three parts after.

Talk of a prequel trilogy had first been floated on the release of *Episode VI: Return of The Jedi* in 1983 and subsequent rumours had been rife, but it was a full ten years before George Lucas would publicly come clean and admit that he was in fact writing all three episodes himself. The idea met with instant universal enthusiasm; not surprising since *Star Wars*, originally turned down by two major studios, had won seven Oscars and, as well as holding on to the crown of the world's biggest grossing movie for twenty years, had also been credited with single-handedly relaunching the science fiction movie genre.

And there were other attractions in returning to the scene of such triumph. The advancement in technology in the intervening two decades now made the sky the limit, and when the original *Star Wars*, with its thousands of fan clubs around the globe, was invigorated by the release of the New Edition video set, it was an intriguing prospect to see what could be achieved this time around. *Star Wars Episode I* would again be distributed by Twentieth Century Fox, who were confident that it would launch a second fabled phenomenon.

Lucas's casting strategy was simple – he hired those actors whom he believed to possess the best ability to portray each respective character. 'I got very fortunate this time,' he declared. 'I found people who seemed to be born to play the role.' Joining McGregor and Liam Neeson, the key players on this new journey into space would include Jake Lloyd, a lively nine year old who would take on the important role of Anakin Skywalker. As the future father of Luke and Princess Leia – and as the character who would eventually become their arch-enemy as the evil

Darth Vader – the director saw in Lloyd signs of the essential charismatic presence that Luke – (Mark Hamill) had conveyed in the original movie. Lucent sixteen-year-old beauty Natalie Portman – whom actor Terence Stamp calls a young Audrey Hepburn – plays the girl queen Amidala who will become Anakin's wife; her inner strength appealed to Lucas. Pernilla August as Shmi Skywalker is Anakin's mother, while Ian McDiarmid returns to take on the mantle of a younger Palpatine, at this stage an ambitious Senator who later becomes the vile and ruthless Emperor.

Cameo roles fell to Sixties screen idol Terence Stamp, famed for his piercingly arresting eyes, as Supreme Chancellor Valorium, the powerful President of the Galaxy. The larger-than-life Brian Blessed as King Boz Naz appears as a gigantic hologram. And American superstar Samuel L Jackson, of *Pulp Fiction* and *Jackie Brown* fame, portrays Mace Windu (Lando Calrissian's father), another wise old Jedi master. No *Star Wars* film could ever be complete without the two famous droids – the beeping, whirling dumpy R2-D2 worked by actor Kenny Baker and the irritatingly correct golden rod C-3PO, which continued to be the responsibility of Anthony Daniels. The several-hundred-year-old master Jedi called Yoda – an appealing mixture of computer generation and puppet – would again be voiced by Frank Oz.

The original film had been shot in the Tikaz National Park, Guatemala, Tunisia and California's Death Valley, with the interior shots filmed at Elstree Studios in Borehamwood, England. *Episode I* took McGregor on a hot and cloudless summer's morning for his first overwhelming day's shooting to the enormous Leavesden Studios with its vast backlot – it was formerly an aerodrome – in Hertfordshire. Later he was to go on location to the Scottish Highlands before travelling abroad to the palace of Regia di Caserta in Italy, to the Mediterranean Sea and the desert wastes of Tozeur, Djerba and Medenine in Tunisia: that country would again stand in for the dusty planet of Tatooine, where Lucas has confirmed that one-third of the new film takes place.

McGregor recalled the trepidation he felt on the eve of his commencing work on the film by admitting that the previous night he had been so scared that he could not sleep. When he arrived for the first cast read-through he had been amazed to find it a casual affair – 'I thought it would be a massive read-through with all the heads of the departments

ABOVE For his third movie under director Danny Boyle, Ewan filmed *A Life Less Ordinary* on location in the vast open spaces of Utah.

ABOVE Ewan and actress Cameron Diaz in the kidnap scene from the movie. During shooting they were to become close friends.

As rock stars, Jonathan Rhys Meyers and Ewan coped well with the demanding gay love scenes in the film.

watching.' Casual atmosphere or not, McGregor remained a little anxious. He later admitted, 'When we did the read-through, I was terrified. Before read-throughs I always imagine I'll do it and then people will say, "Look, I'm sorry Ewan, but this just isn't going to work out." But that didn't happen.'

Seeing the hive of activity at Leavesden Studios made a big impression on McGregor though and his delight in no small way came from seeing a wide variety of oh-so-familiar props. 'I was actually screaming out loud,' he admitted, adding, 'Thank God there were no stormtroopers there at that time or I would have been out of control. I always wanted to be in a stormtrooper outfit. They're the sexiest uniform that's ever been in the movies.'

Nothing intrigues more than a fine veil of secrecy thrown over filming. In this case it resembled a thick blanket. George Lucas had insisted that the main cast and crew were bound fast by cast-iron non-disclosure contracts that would legally prohibit discussion of the film's plot or characters. It is further rumoured that large bonuses were dangled before particular people as further incentive to stay tight-lipped. Of the official contracts McGregor confirms, 'I've had to sign *so* many bits of paper you just wouldn't believe it.' He admits that such a condition is not the norm, but he well appreciates the need for such precautions in this case. 'The second anything's divulged it's straight onto the Internet,' he says. He has developed a formula for use when questioned about *Star Wars*, 'I can't tell you anything about that.'

The film press, however, were determined not to be entirely thwarted. In addition to scrutinising parts IV, V and VI for clues that could backdate events, piece by piece they believed they were winkling out at least the outline of the plot. It has to be noted that not only could George Lucas alter story lines if unhappy with the result, so determined is he to play his cards close to his chest that he could also choose to significantly change tack if any major pillar of the plot did fall into the public domain. It is alleged that he has made up decoy scripts with bogus plotlines to throw any serious snoopers off the scent. However, according to the latest word, the prequel is said to begin thirty years before the events of *Episode IV*, in a time when the Galaxy is ruled by the Republic, a democratic alliance held together by a clutch of intergalactic Senators with the strong-arm support of the Jedi Knights, a mystical order which for countless centuries have been the guardians of peace and justice. *Episode I*, with the responsibility of mapping out characters and explaining the credo of the Jedi, promises to be as George Lucas has suggested: similar to the fun action-adventure of the existing trio of films, but at the same time marking the beginnings of a far darker trilogy.

'It is about Kenobi as a young man,' the director let out. And it is thought to brim with plotting and intrigue as it deals with the power-hungry Senator Palpatine and the rise of the Empire as the old Republic is overthrown. A massacre of the Jedi order apparently leaves Qui-Gon Jinn and Obi-Wan Kenobi the only survivors of their kind. The two flee to Tatooine which is where Obi-Wan meets and rescues Anakin Skywalker, whose mother and sister have been slain. As Palpatine seeks the seductive alternative attractions of the dark side of The Force – the energy that bonds the galaxy and from which a Jedi draws his power – McGregor's and Neeson's characters head to an underwater world, said to be called Gunga, to seek help.

An explosive good-versus-evil battle to try to save the Republic in the submerged kingdom provides a mind-boggling finale with chariot races; a blitz of light-sabre duels, metal skeletons and other creatures such as squid people. With its pivotal themes of betrayal and conflict, in the overall schemes of things the trilogy will clearly have to embrace the story of Anakin Skywalker growing up and explore why he becomes Darth Vader. It is also tentatively suggested that the story will examine a potential love triangle between Obi-Wan, Anakin and the beautiful and spirited Queen Amidala. In the pecking order Qui-Gon Jinn (Neeson), himself below Yoda, is the master Jedi training McGregor's Obi-Wan in the ways of the Force which includes instilling in him a Samurai-style code of ethics. As is already established, Kenobi subsequently teaches Anakin Skywalker before he chooses evil over good.

Amidst all the avid conjecture surrounding the plot, only one thing seems certain. The main sketch of the story that George Lucas originally outlined in the early-to-mid Seventies will, in essence, remain the same, regardless of how he has chosen to interpret it. 'Basically,' he says, 'the story is what the story is, even though it was written twenty-five years ago. It's like reworking a novel.' With the project reportedly costing between

$115–$125 million it is said to include the Jedi-friendly creature Jar Jar Binks, such familiar and well loved entities as Sand People, Banthas, Wookies and over 1,500 visual effects. Jabba the Hutt and Boba Fett also make return appearances.

In the absence of concrete facts, rumours continued to evolve based on snippets of information as the filming progressed throughout the summer. One nugget was that actress Carrie Fisher, who played Princess Leia, the feisty heroine of the original three movies, had been consulted to revise the dialogue for the new film's female characters. An unnamed source supposedly close to the director was quoted as saying of Fisher, 'She doesn't believe that women in movies should stand around and wait for the guy to rescue them.'

In *Episode I* there were to be decided parallels in characterisation with the original, with Liam Neeson taking on the Alec Guinness role of the worldly-wise master Jedi and McGregor as the reckless, rebellious, impatient pupil. George Lucas felt that he had found in the Ballymena-born Neeson the exact degree of nobility and quiet strength required. 'You think, where are you going to find another Alec Guinness?' queried Lucas. 'But Liam is the guy.'

Unlike the innocent, obedient Luke Skywalker, however, McGregor's Obi-Wan is said to more closely resemble Harrison Ford's roguish Han Solo persona – a far more colourful hook to get a hold of. It's certainly what the director was looking for in casting. 'Ewan is the perfect Harrison Ford, but he's also a great young Alec Guinness. He's extremely relaxed and very strong. All the things that Guinness is.'

Sir Alec Guinness, whose films include the Ealing comedies *Kind Hearts And Coronets* and *The Ladykillers*, as well as *The Bridge On The River Kwai*, had provided a touch of dignity and class in *Star Wars* in 1977 as old Obi-Wan Kenobi with his white hair, neat beard and flowing robes, a master Jedi now living quietly as a hermit beyond the Dune Sea on Tatooine. Sir Alec has one of the most distinctive voices in the business. And it was on this same voice that McGregor focused a lot of his attention during preparation for the new movie.

Although Ben Kenobi allowed himself to be killed in a light-sabre duel with his former pupil Darth Vader in the original *Star Wars* film, he goes on to appear at vital moments in hologram form in both sequels and as a result fans of the trilogy have had his comforting tones and image cemented for years into their consciousness. For McGregor this made his job to time-warp Obi-Wan back to his days as a virile young dashing knight an even bigger responsibility. 'It was a really exciting task to be able to take on someone who's legendary,' he said, but it was also a task that would prove problematic in several ways.

McGregor was caught in something of a cleft stick. On the one hand he was reluctant to ape another actor's performance in a role, but on the other hand he had a definite duty to create authentic continuity. His respect for Alec Guinness was apparent, 'To play the young Alec Guinness is an incredible honour. He's done some of the most incredible movie work', but he did not approach the veteran star to discuss the character. Instead he concentrated on watching existing footage of both actor and character. Said McGregor, 'I've been watching loads of Alec Guinness's old movies. Not to try and imitate him in any way, but just to try to catch a flavour of inflections and vocal mannerisms, some looks that I thought might work here and there. After all, I'm meant to *be* Obi-Wan Kenobi and you have to be able to see that I would eventually become him.' He went on, 'That was the challenge really, more than who the Jedi are or what makes him tick. The step between the end of *Episode III* and the beginning of *Episode IV* has to be one that you can believe. It's a leap of faith that I become him.'

As a kid McGregor had been word-perfect on the *Star Wars* dialogue, but now he had to sit through repeated video viewings, this time scrutinising the older actor at work, listening hard and trying to get the voice right. He quickly identified the chief problem of trying to sound like a *young* Alec Guinness. 'It is a voice most people associate with an old man,' he explained, 'and to put it into a young person's body is quite weird. I've been doing a lot of dialogue coaching to try and get a younger-sounding version of his voice. It's quite a trick to imagine what it sounded like, because in a lot of his younger films he's playing with an accent anyway. It's important that we match but I don't know if it worked or not. I'll find out in a couple of years,' he would say with bald candour.

He also had other aspects of the character to prepare. 'Before we started I worked a lot with Nick Gillard, a stunt coordinator in London. He's a really nice guy and doesn't try to be butch. A lot of stunt men just waste film time by justifying their presence on the set. As I'm playing a Jedi Knight, I did not want to seem ineffective and he gave me lots of confidence.'

It was an important aspect of the film to get right, for according to McGregor the battle or fight sequences in the new movie are significantly more lively. 'I think the fighting in this film is much grungier than the stuff in the first three. It's slightly more aggressive, more ferocious and faster. It's rather violent, quite tasty fighting.' A firm departure that he personally felt was completely warranted. He reflected, 'There is a lot of talk in *Episodes IV–VI* about what the Jedi used to be like and yet you never know what they're really about. So you see us kick some butt in this film. We're jumping all over the place.' He described it as unlike any other kind of fighting that he had done before. 'It's lightsaber fighting, a skill of its own. I get to be flash. When I'm fighting I do lots of twists and spins and twirls and showing off a bit.' His impressive robes as Obi-Wan Kenobi did not always prove helpful to these energetic displays. Of his heavy cloak McGregor recalled, 'It's so huge. You're always falling over it. Fighting in it, my sword's going up my sleeve and under my cloak. It looks great and it's a great idea on paper, but it's pretty hard to wear.'

Filming itself held other challenges. It was the first time McGregor would be required to act against a blue screen – a demanding process for any actor who has to imagine action going on around him that will in fact be added in later by special effects. Mark Hamill famously remarked of the first *Star Wars*, 'Acting in this movie I felt like a raisin in a giant fruit salad and I didn't even know who the coconuts or the canteloupes were.' And McGregor's *A Life Less Ordinary* co-star Cameron Diaz could also sympathise, having experienced blue-screen acting in *The Mask*. It was remarkably difficult work, she would stress, pointing out bluntly, 'you feel like an asshole'. McGregor himself says, 'It was much more tiring and was hard because the pretending is so much of it.' He reveals, 'Because everyone's attention is on so many other things – what the background is going to be, what's going on in the foreground – I think it would be very easy to put in a very bad performance and it would be easy to get away with it.'

He was certainly beginning to have ambivalent feelings about the whole process: he was seeing for himself just what Denis Lawson had warned him of. 'Making this kind of film *is* tedious,' he confirms. 'It's so technical. You would be hanging around for days, so it was quite boring. There's no character discovery to be had. It's just a lot of frowning and that's about it really. It was very weird. The Jedi Knights have got a sense of what's going to happen so they don't freak out or panic or anything. You just have to get to your mark then hope all the special effects people will do the rest.' But with the same breath he confesses, 'It was a slog – but every so often during the day I would have a *Star Wars* moment. I'd go, "Whoop! Fuckin' *Star Wars!* Whoop!" '

He also connected well with George Lucas. 'He was great,' says McGregor. 'I really enjoyed working with him. He's a lovely man. He likes a good chat. He'll talk to you for hours about his world and what goes on in it. He's kind of like a king – not in the way he behaves, but just because he lives in his own world. His ranch – the Skywalker Ranch – is built in this big valley in Northern California and he owns the valley. He's in charge of so many different things. He's the boss.'

However, there were times when actor and director saw aspects of the Obi-Wan Kenobi character in different lights. McGregor explains, 'George didn't think the Jedi was quite like the way I perceived him and every time I tried to put in a bit of a joke or something, he would say, "Cut that smile out." ' McGregor jokes about filming *Star Wars*, 'I was looking for the right moment to drop my Jedi knickers and pull out my real lightsaber. By now my audience will appreciate I have nothing to be ashamed of.'

It thrilled him, too, to see characters so familiar to him in cinema terms 'coming alive', and in this he was not alone. Ian McDiarmid reveals, 'A lot of us used to have to pinch ourselves to remind ourselves of what we were involved in.' Of McGregor, he observes, 'It took him back to when he was a kid, I think.'

Using a lightsaber, the elegant weapon of a Jedi warrior, came top of McGregor's list of the thrills that this role provided for him. 'Man, if they were real they'd be bloody lethal,' he later gasped. 'The ones we're using are seriously dodgy as it is.' Just prior to the film's release he was able to reveal how it felt to be presented with his first lightsaber on set. 'A man from props came up and took me into the room. There were sixty guys standing about and he came out, dead secretive, with this big wooden box with two padlocks on and the secrecy was incredible. He unlocked it, asked me if I was ready – and inlaid in black felt there were these nine or ten lightsaber handles. And I just about really shat myself. And I took out these precious things and chose my handle and realised how much these things were ingrown in the psyche. I grew up on them.' He experienced a very similar reaction when, towards the end of 1998, George Lucas permitted McGregor to view some rough-cuts from the movie. The sight of himself cutting a dash with his lightsaber now that the special effects had been added nearly knocked McGregor out. 'Oooh!' he exclaims. 'I nearly shat myself! I just about died with excitement. I mean, no one gets to do that – but I did.'

It was, in fact, wielding a lightsaber that brought it home to him that he was acting out a childhood dream. 'I had my own lightsaber. Wow! That was mad! It's the most exciting thing I've ever known. I can't have it in my hand and not give it a few twirls. There's nothing cooler than being a Jedi Knight. It's so familiar, wearing all the Jedi stuff, the clogs and so on. It's very peculiar doing it. I had a great time. It certainly is an honour.'

When filming took place at Leavesden Studios it had an added bonus; it meant that he could commute from home five days a week. McGregor recalls how his excitement at that time spilled over into his domestic situation. 'When I first met R2-D2, I almost went down on the ground. It was a bit like meeting the Queen – it was a very honoured moment. I went home one day and my wife was sitting with a lot of her mates and I go, "I worked with R2-D2 today!" and they all looked at me and went, "Who?" I guess it's a boy's thing. The chicks just don't get it.'

Although McGregor could not reveal anything about his scenes with the droid, he was thrilled at meeting its operator Kenny Baker. 'There he was again,' he said, 'doing it twenty years later, being lowered into R2-D2. How weird it was for him.' As for Baker, he says, 'I found Ewan a very pleasant, happy-go-lucky and easy kind of guy. The schedule was really hectic. We worked till late after having had to be up at 4.00 am, so there was not a great deal of time left for socialising. It was a happy production though and all I can tell you is that Ewan was delighted to be playing Obi-Wan Kenobi and that he is *very* good in the role.'

The director corroborates Kenny Baker's view that a sense of contentment pervaded the set. The historic moment when they began shooting on the first day had also been an emotional one, with its tense mix of anticipation and nerves; the air was thick with expectancy. McGregor was aware of it at once: 'The place was buzzing before we started filming: you could feel it as soon as you walked in. But, during shooting, Lucas revealed, 'I feel lucky every day that everybody's here. There's a lot of enthusiasm' – which clearly stemmed from the fact that virtually all of the cast members had been dying to be part of this new trilogy. As Lucas would remark, no one had had to have their arm metaphorically twisted to be in the film. And Liam Neeson talked of all the cast bonding in a really good way. For his part, Ewan revealed that although they all worked what he called 'ridiculously long' hours, they all loved it. 'Nobody would be anywhere else,' he maintained, recalling that he had got to the point when he would sit in the studio and play backgammon after work because he was reluctant to leave the set.

Like McGregor, Neeson too felt slightly disorientated by the blue-screen element. 'When the camera is on me it's really hard to focus my eyes on something that's not there without having a sort of blank gaze.' However, he stresses that everyone soon got used to it and that he personally found it quite a liberating experience – allowing his imagination the sort of full rein enjoyed as a child. It did, he states, encourage new levels of inventiveness.

This semi-regression to childhood days – pretending to enact battles – on occasion meant personally providing full sound effects. Liam reveals, 'The first time Ewan and I had to do any lightsaber work, we started making the lightsaber noises and soon felt a bit silly.' They quickly realised that they did not in fact have to compensate for what was not yet there.

Ultimately McGregor revealed of the film, 'It's completely different to anything I've done before in my life.' He had, till now, been accustomed to arriving on set and shooting a scene with the other actors in that take; although the footage would then be taken away and edited, what was filmed that day would appear like that, more or less in the movie. 'With *Star Wars*,' he explained, 'you shoot a scene, they take it away and do different things to it and change it around, *then* stick it in the movie.' He went on, 'It's kind of like starting again. And the scale of it? I've never done a big movie like that before either. You can see how enchanting that would be.'

There were, however, times when it was difficult to find enchantment in the intense hard work required to make such a colossal movie on such a punishing schedule: the first to operate on a twenty-four hour basis. Undoubtedly such a rigorous timetable enabled the film-makers to keep on schedule, but it meant that, after putting in twelve hours of filming, George Lucas then had to transmit the day's rushes via a satellite to the famous special effects' maestros ILM (Industrial Light and Magic) in America. Using the latest and most sophisticated technology they worked their technical wizardry to incorporate computer-generated creatures and virtual backgrounds into this rough footage through the night hours, before beaming the results back the same way to the director, ready for the next day's shoot.

Yet all the advanced technology in the world was of no assistance when the production fell spectacularly foul of Mother Nature when shooting in Tunisia. After weeks of sweltering in the scorching heat, the area was hit by a violent sandstorm which almost wrecked the entire expensive set. Costumes and costly props were rendered write-offs. McGregor has vivid memories of it, although he witnessed it from the safety of being inside the hotel where he was staying. 'We saw this wall of sand coming towards us. When it hit us the lightning was going right across the sky – it was awesome.' But where the actor was thunderstruck, the director was completely unfazed; almost pleased. McGregor later recalled that they had naturally assumed that this disastrous happening would render the cast redundant for a few days while the damage was repaired, and he expected to find George Lucas less than happy. In fact, as McGregor recalled, 'George said, "Oh, this is a *good* omen." We said, "What?" He said, "This happened in the first one and this is a good thing that we've had our set destroyed." '

Such dramas aside, filming continued elsewhere until the set was rebuilt and principal photography wrapped on 26 September and, as Ian McDiarmid recalls, it ended on a high note. 'George waited for the final moments to press the special effects, so that it finished with a light show and a bit of a bang. I thought that was a good showman's touch.' Lucas and company then packed up and returned to their base in San Rafael, California to begin the lengthy and complicated post-production process on *Episode I*. The pre-production and design stages on *Episode II* and

crew and the gaffer, and stardom quite clearly hadn't at all gone to his head. The first thing I noticed about him was that he is very much one of the lads.'

Philip Jackson had found exactly the same. 'The most interesting thing for me was working with Ewan that second time. He had done such a lot in between and I wondered if he would have changed. But he hadn't. If anything he was more open and generous than ever. Nothing had turned his head, which I thought was amazing in the circumstances. We spent much more time together this time around than we did when we had filmed *Brassed Off*. In fact, along with Ewan's driver Steve Timms we made up an inseparable threesome.'

Scarborough, very popular with English tourists, proved to be both a welcoming town and a place which scored a hit with the cast. Bridlington-born director Mark Herman had scouted seaside towns from North Shields to Skegness before settling on Scarborough to stand in for the fictional town in the movie. 'All these east coast towns looked the same,' he said, 'but Scarborough had a certain interesting architecture. It's the hill and the cliff which makes it visually more interesting.' The robust fresh sea air certainly appealed to McGregor, who finds something magical in such coastal resorts, he enjoyed playing the one-arm bandits in the countless packed and noisy slot-machine arcades. 'I really like it up here,' he said. 'It's very beautiful.' Several locals would take part as extras in the film and there was a general air of good humour, even when a misunderstanding by the local police ruined a morning's work.

A vigilant police officer on patrol who had not been informed of the shooting schedule identified what he believed to be two suspicious-looking vehicles crawling slowly – one flashing hazard-warning lights – along a quiet road early one Sunday morning. Doing his duty, he stopped the cars to question their occupants – only to discover that he had just gatecrashed a scene in a movie and in the process spoiled over three hours of filming. The producers, who might reasonably have been expected to be furious since they had provided the local constabulary with details of their shooting schedules, took it all in good part.

Being hot off the set of the latest *Star Wars* movie made McGregor an even bigger magnet to the regional media; as Britain's fastest rising star he was required to have immense patience with the inevitable persistent attentions of the Press. 'It's really nice to come back to a small film crew,' he revealed, confirming that he was having a great time. A strong sense of camaraderie built up during the month's shoot. Brenda Blethyn said, 'It's a joy to be working with such a great piece. It's so exciting and Jane Horrocks is like a breath of fresh air. It's very nice indeed to play opposite Ewan McGregor,' she added. 'And Michael Caine.' And it was the famous cockney actor Caine who had most impressed McGregor. Says Philip Jackson, 'Ewan had no actual scenes with Michael but he was *so* overawed about working on the same film as him. He came right up to me once, bright-eyed and breathless, and said, "I've just been chatting with Michael Caine!" And I told him, "Well, hang on lad. Just think what you've done!" '

The cast were determined not to behave like prima donnas when they were not filming and regularly took themselves out on the town. For McGregor and Jackson this usually meant finding a congenial pub for a few beers. Says Jackson, 'We went off out all the time. Ewan goes about as if he isn't famous at all and most of the time it all went fine. There were a couple of difficult Friday nights when some guys with a drink in tried to hassle him but he handled them well. He's forever patient, you see, and will sign autographs, have his photo taken and so on. And that makes a difference.'

McGregor's practice of deliberately remaining unfettered by his celebrity status is all part of his insistence in leading as normal an off-screen life as possible. But if he steadfastly refused to be impressed by his fame, others were not at all reticent at recognising it, as he discovered when Ewan-mania hit Scarborough town. Philip Jackson explains. 'While we were filming there the local newspaper wanted to do a spread and one night after it had appeared in the paper we were out walking and from a distance, round a corner, we heard these girls chanting "Ewan McGregor! Ewan McGregor!" And they hadn't even see us. We carried on round the corner and they saw him then and went completely berserk. He got mobbed like that a lot – but there again he is really game and just handles it.'

It was well known by now that Ewan McGregor had just finished film-ing the latest *Star Wars* movie and the fever was mounting. But in addition to the teenage girls who wanted to drool over him and the boys who wanted to drink with him, there was a huge *Star Wars* fan who was simply desperate to meet him – and who went to ingenious lengths to achieve his goal.

Seven-year-old Scarborough schoolboy Simon Franklin had discovered that McGregor, whom he knew from a space magazine was to be the new young Obi-Wan Kenobi, was part of the cast of a film to be shot in his home town. He wanted passionately to get in touch with the star. Unaided he wrote an extraordinarily clever open letter to McGregor inviting him to tea, with intentions of sending it to the local newspaper, the *Scarborough Evening News*. His mother, Nicky Franklin, a student of graphic design and photography, had auditioned for – and won – a part as an extra in *Little Voice* and she recalls, 'Simon had gone ahead and written a letter on the computer and had it all typed up before he showed it to me. He gave it to me, asking if I could give it to Ewan on the film set. I said, "Hey, wait a minute, I'm only an extra. I probably will never meet him." '

After making her son hand-write the letter she telephoned the local newspaper to see if they could let her know where the cast were staying and explaining about Simon's letter. 'They were so impressed by the letter,' she remembers, 'that they ran a piece about it in their paper and sent a photographer round to picture Simon with the mountain of his *Star Wars* stuff.'

The open letter appeared in the *Evening News* days after filming had begun and soon after Nicky managed to discover where the crew were currently working. 'We found out they were making a set at Scarborough Castle,' she says. 'The location manager was called Mark Herbert and the men told us to come back on Monday.' With a day off school specially Simon, with his mother, turned up at 6.00 am and the young boy raced onto the set to track down Herbert. The locations manager accepted a copy of the newspaper and the child's letter and promised to see what could be done.

Touched and very impressed by Simon's erudite letter, McGregor was more than happy to meet the boy. Says Nicky, 'Mark Herbert walked up to us with this guy who immediately bent down and began talking to Simon. I didn't recognise that it was Ewan McGregor.'

She goes on, 'He was absolutely lovely to Simon and made him feel very important. His little face just lit up. A seven-year-old meeting his hero! Simon had been clasping his *Star Wars* book all day tightly to his chest but he let Ewan see it, who autographed it for him. Now it's locked away and none of us gets to see it. The whole thing was only about ten minutes as they needed Ewan back on set. There were other fans – girls who had gathered nearby hoping to get him to sign autographs – which he did, he was nice to everyone, but he paid all of his attention to Simon before he went to the others and I really appeciated that.'

Fairly bursting with glee, Simon told the reporter for the *Evening News* how McGregor had hugged him and told him how much he thought of his letter. 'I was very excited,' said Simon. 'It made my day.' He also revealed what his hero had written in his precious book. It reads, *Dear Simon, Och aye The Force! Good to meet you mate. May The Force Be With You. Signed Ewan McGregor (the young Obi-Wan Kenobi).*

As Simon Franklin headed home, his dream come true, McGregor returned to work. Location filming ended on 16 November when, along with the rest of the cast and crew, he left Scarborough. In all filming for *Little Voice* would take nine weeks, as work continued at studios in Twickenham, but it was over for McGregor. His scenes had been crammed into the first month to enable him to meet his next commitment.

It had been a special pleasure for him to work for a second time with director Mark Herman, who had big hopes for the success of the film, which would open the London Film Festival on 5 November 1998. 'Most of my work has been done in the writing and the casting,' he said. 'With a cast like this, the directing just becomes making it visually interesting.'

Having filmed *Star Wars* and *Little Voice* almost back-to-back, McGregor would have very little time before he was due to climb into yet another new role. Philip Jackson had attested to how unchanged he had found the young man – his continued willingness to meet and please his fans had been proved in Scarborough – but others had believed for months that they could detect something different about McGregor.

In a young performer's early days the oxygen of publicity is vital and McGregor had wisely been no exception in welcoming exposure. Over the years he had become adept at handling promotion and interviews usually in a jokey style and had effortlessly won over numerous journalists with his relaxed charm and professionalism. Indeed, the effect of his charm on female reporters could often be so pronounced as to be apparent in the features they subsequently wrote – one particular journalist later waxed lyrical about 'the laser beam of light shooting out from his pale blue eyes'. He inadvertantly endeared himself to others by cutting short a session in order to play hide and seek in the lounge with his little daughter. Not that he was ever too much of a pussycat – in familiarly blunt fashion he once issued a colourful threat. An interviewer had teased him by threatening to write that Ewan had somehow found salvation in his domestic bliss – to which McGregor riposted, 'If I see those words in quotes, I'm gonna roll up the magazine and come and shove it right up your arse!'

But circumstances inevitably alter the more successful an actor becomes. Some commentators wonder if McGregor has truly yet appreciated just how *Star Wars* will affect life as he knows it; whether he has any real conception of the heights to which he will be rocketed. McGregor has refuted as 'shite' claims in one newspaper that he had become addicted to fame and that suddenly, after landing the Obi-Wan Kenobi role, he had raised the drawbridge on the hitherto liberal access he had permitted the Press. And certainly he has by no means ceased to give interviews, nor has he become a recluse; in 1997 he had reportedly only just begun to feel occasionally uneasy whilst travelling on the London Underground.

However, that summer a sea change was believed detectable by more than one journalist seeking to encroach on some of his now desperately rationed free time and by autumn McGregor was himself talking openly of the 'mistake' he felt he had made in the past by being so willing and open. Blaming inexperience, he said he had felt duty-bound for a long time to answer any question put to him, no matter how probing. Because of this, he had frequently ended up revealing more about himself than he was, on reflection, comfortable with, with the result that his private life no longer seemed to belong to him. He confessed that, sometimes, this had left him feeling temporarily 'empty and depressed'. 'Actually, interviews can make me feel insecure. People feel they have the right to ask you absolutely anything. They say, "How do you show your romantic side to your wife?" And I reply, "Absolutely none of your fucking business." And they get annoyed. I start thinking, "*Is* my family life really secure, like I think it is?" '

It is natural that the more mature McGregor would redraw his strategy and, having just completed a film which would send his stock soaring into orbit, there was no better time to do so. It was a question of self-preservation. If he had a duty, he now believed it was to protect the privacy of himself and his family.

One step likely to assist in enabling him to do this was to relocate. His London agent Lindy King revealed, 'For *Trainspotting* Ewan got next to nothing. For *Velvet Goldmine* he got ten times that. And for *Star Wars* – well, he'll get ten times that again.' The fruits of his rapidly-rising profile – not to mention the extremely generous pay cheque for the *Star Wars* films – had helped purchase a luxury house in London's fashionable St John's Wood, said to have cost in the region of £1.25 million. The new address was much in keeping with his latest accolade – that of being named one of the ten most powerful players in the British film industry. He would seek to confirm this status in his next role; he was next due to portray, not an honourable Jedi Knight, but a young high-flier who fell to earth dramatically – and helped bring the world's oldest merchant bank crashing down with him.

CHAPTER 11

Rogue Impulses

FILMING FOR *Rogue Trader* began in late November 1997. It would be McGregor's first taste of the responsibility of portraying a real, living person.

Prior to *Rogue Trader*'s release McGregor revealed, 'It was fascinating to bury yourself in the world of finance, which I know nothing about. I learned to say things convincingly without understanding them. I could watch the real person on a video. It was about becoming someone, rather than creating someone.'

The movie was based on the book of the same name, the bestselling autobiography of Englishman Nick Leeson, the futures trader who, on 2 December 1995, was sentenced to six and a half years in jail to be served in the tough regime of Changi prison in Singapore for his part in the spectacular financial collapse of the 200-year-old Barings Bank. The scandal had made shock headline news around the world at the start of that year.

Opposite McGregor as Nick Leeson's wife – air hostess Lisa – would be Anna Friel, the Lancashire-born actress whose credits numbered several television soaps, including *Coronation Street, Emmerdale, Brookside* and *Medics*, and the 1998 wartime weepie *Land Girls*. The £8 million film, to be fully funded by Granada TV, would depict Leeson and the events which led to his racking up debts of £850 million, triggering the downfall of Barings Bank, his flight from Singapore and his capture, arrest, trial and eventual imprisonment. The director in charge of this fast-moving and astonishing tale – he also adapted the screenplay – was to be James Dearden, writer of the 1987 box office sensation *Fatal Attraction*.

Leeson's white-collar crime, his dramatic fall from grace, and how this drastic financial collapse had ever been possible, fascinated millions around the world. Inevitably the interest sparked speculation of a possible film, although at first such a prospect looked likely to be ruled out when it was reported in the Press that a writ had been served in Britain designed to deny Nick Leeson the chance to profit from his notoriety. There would be no Hollywood film of his life and exploits as had been claimed. A movie would also be an impossibility unless it was committed to revealing only the exact truth behind the collapse of Barings. But veteran television interviewer Sir David Frost, who had gone to interview Leeson in a Frankfurt jail soon after the man's arrest, could not shake the disgraced futures trader's story from his mind.

During the nine months that Leeson had been incarcerated in this Frankfurt jail awaiting extradition he had occupied his time by writing his autobiography. Frost – with his own company, Paradine Productions – moved to buy the film rights to this book. 'I was absolutely fascinated by the man, his wife and every aspect of this incredible situation. I somehow knew I wanted to make a film out of the story.'

David Frost had not produced a film for twenty years and then it had been a vastly different type of project – *The Slipper And The Rose*, a family musical based on the story of Cinderella. There would be no fairytale ending to this story, but it was one which Frost felt would make for a riveting movie. He was especially struck by what he believed was the integral issue of class resonating throughout the whole sorry saga. 'There is something about the whole thing of Nick Leeson being a barrow–boy trader and not a member of Boodles or a regular at the Hunt Ball,' said Frost, who became *Rogue Trader*'s executive producer.

McGregor led the cast when filming, newly underway, moved to scenes at Gatwick airport on 28 November. Production was concentrated in and around the capital until Christmas, after which the cast and crew debunked to Malaysia and Singapore where filming continued into January 1998.

The film's producer Paul Raphael described the movie. 'It is a roller-coaster of a film about a streetwise guy who just got way out of his depth.'

Adopting an Essex accent, McGregor had also in portraying this outwardly confident man to reveal a guy totally preoccupied with his high-pressure job to the exclusion of all else. Lisa Leeson once said of her husband, 'He wanted to recoup. If only the Kobe earthquake hadn't happened. Someone told me that the market is soaring now and that Nick would have made millions. He could have been a hero.'

There was nothing remotely heroic, however, about languishing in a foreign jail and this aspect of it would bother McGregor from the out-set. Nick Leeson was not permitted visitors other than family members but director James Dearden managed to wangle one visit to talk to the subject of his film. McGregor, on the other hand, was flatly denied per-mission to set foot inside Changi prison and this came as a huge relief to him. 'I don't want to have an opinion about [Leeson] because people are very black and white about the case. Some people think he's a com-plete animal, and some people think he's a victim. I want to play it in the middle.'

But there was more to McGregor's relief than that. He found himself acutely uncomfortable with the thought of talking to a man banged up in such basic conditions. What on earth could he possibly say to Leeson that was not unfeeling; an actor who lived in the lap of luxury, while the pris-oner had nothing more to look forward to than a rush mat in a claustro-phobic cell? In the latter stages, when the cast was on location in Singapore itself, McGregor said, 'It isn't easy. We're all swanning around, eating lunch and having a good time – and he's in jail just around the cor-ner.' But if he was distressed by this angle of portraying Leeson, other aspects did not bother him at all. In 1994, just months before his arrest for fraud, the City whizzkid had fallen foul of the authorities for a different kind of offence when he was arrested for dropping his trousers and mooning to three air hostesses. Ever the exhibitionist, McGregor spoke of handling this moment on screen. 'Showing my arse doesn't mean anything to me. I couldn't care less about it.' He added that, in general, 'Filming is going very well.'

As newscaster Jon Snow can vouch, McGregor's spirits were indeed high. 'I did an interview with Ewan on the set of *Rogue Trader* and he was wearing Nick Leeson's actual work tie, which he was delighted about, and he was very enthusiastic about the film.' Also wearing a distinctive trader's striped blazer McGregor spoke to the newscaster and reporter of his past scare with his daughter's health, as well as his concern at the number of movies he had made which were stacking up in the distribution pipeline.

Executive producer Sir David Frost was more than happy to leave the actual making of the movie to James Dearden. As he put it himself, his responsibility had been to make sure that the project got off the ground. And in spring 1998, when the movie moved into the post-production phase, Frost saw his first glimpse of the results. He told a journalist, 'I've just seen the rushes. I knew that Ewan would be superb and Anna [Friel] too gives an incredible performance as his wife. It's very strong.'

McGregor was to experience something of the ruthlessness of film-making on completion of *Rogue Trader*. 'It was a classic case of breaking your balls for someone on a film and then never hearing from them again after the editing.'

Nevertheless, anticipation was high for the success of *Rogue Trader*, with Paul Raphael optimistically declaring, 'I hope we can get Nick Leeson along to the premiere. That would be wonderful.' Whether that was at all practical was extremely debatable when, in July 1998, came the sad news that Nick Leeson was in very poor health, suffering from cancer. Applications were made for an early release on compassionate grounds.

On the film front too there was soon a potential cloud threatening to hover. In the summer of 1997 the *Sunday Times* had reported news of a possible snag set to rain on *Rogue Trader*'s parade in the shape of another film version of the Barings Bank collapse, being prepared under wraps by the BBC. Claims emerged that this production was to benefit from assistance given by former Barings executives and that, significantly, the BBC film would be ready well before James Dearden's. Were *Rogue Trader* to come out after the BBC film it was felt that it could only suffer commercially; in addition, the BBC version of the same story was thought to, as the paper put it, 'jar in key essentials with Leeson's own account'. Not, of course, that any of this was within McGregor's control. He had fulfilled his obligations and it was time to move on.

But first he would take time out to help actors less busy or less fortunate than himself. Like many actors McGregor has had his fair share of voiceover work, including an in-flight information film for Virgin

Airways. Said McGregor, soon after *Trainspotting* took the cinemas by storm, 'I don't really need to be doing [voiceovers] any more.' But he pointed out that his voiceover agents dated back to his early days; because he appreciated their efforts, he said, he continued to take on this kind of work. And just as his voice was deemed to be an attractive asset, so too in early 1998 was his face – as Isla Blair explained.

'I am the chairperson of a welfare committee called ACT – Actors' Charitable Trust – of which Richard Attenborough is the president, and Ewan has agreed along with Kate Winslet to be among those photographed for a poster campaign to bring young people's attention to this much-needed charity. The Trust looks after actors who, for whatever reason, hit hard times, which in this business is a very real problem. People often castigate actors for their egos but really we are a supportive and helpful group of people. We take great pride when one of our lot, like Ewan, does so well. And we appreciate Ewan agreeing to be one of the young faces to help our cause.'

McGregor has always had deeply-held views on those movies with truly astronomical budgets. He acknowledges that, when these films become global smash hits and rake in colossal sums of money, in turn a great deal of investment is poured back into the industry. But he still considers it obscene that the amount of money spent on making a single blockbuster movie could practically cover the cost of feeding a Third World country and he has not been slow to voice these feelings. He once famously decried big budget movies as 'sick, a disgrace. Anyone who's involved with that kind of film-making should be ashamed of themselves,' he declared. However, this is not a universally held opinion in a highly competitive business where the pressure to provide ever-more elaborate and authentic settings is immense.

By the time McGregor finished filming *Rogue Trader* in January 1998 rumours had been reverberating for some time that McGregor might be taking steps to try to combat the increasing domination of Hollywood blockbusters. At the Cannes Film Festival nine months previously, the Natural Nylon production company had been officially launched; Ewan McGregor and a band of his friends were adding a new string to their professional bows.

A number of actors have, over the years, gone down this same route into production. While it is sensible to expand one's interests in such a fickle business, starting up a production company is considered to be a risky venture. However, it does open up new freedoms; there is scope to develop original ideas. It cuts out much of the need for the services provided by high-priced agencies – and also affords the opportunity for the actors behind the company to cast themselves in the best roles. McGregor explained, 'It's called Natural Nylon. My friend Jude Law came up with the name while he was in New York. Nylon stands for the letters in New York and London. Natural Nylon? It's a contradiction in terms, isn't it? Anyway, it's formed by me, Jude, Sadie Frost, Jonny Lee Miller and Sean Pertwee.'

The actors revealed that they had been inspired to take this step by the formation in 1919 of United Artists, a studio set up by Charlie Chaplin, Douglas Fairbanks, Mary Pickford and director D W Griffith to challenge the dominance of the established all-powerful Hollywood distributors. In mid-December 1997 it was announced that Natural Nylon was now a £60.5 million production company which had received backing from BBC Films and giant companies including Trademark, Alliance, Polygram Filmed Entertainment and Sony Pictures. They had sufficient backing for ten films, most of which will be shot in Britain. It would be their policy to pool their respective talents in working on these projects themselves, as well as making movies for other people. Natural Nylon hopes to try and boost the homegrown movie industry and prevent the debilitating migration of talent across the sea, whilst aiming to make international hits. Sadie Frost – who played Lucy in the 1992 film by Francis Ford Coppola, *Bram Stoker's Dracula* and was then out of the spotlight for five years – says, 'For years I was frustrated by the roles I was sent and Natural Nylon is a way of taking some control again.' Film executive Kevin Loader of The Bridge, which is assisting in funding a number of Natural Nylon's projects, told reporters, 'There is a real buzz about them in Los Angeles before people have woken up to them properly in Britain.'

While McGregor's involvement in Natural Nylon will clearly not prevent him from working with other companies he, like his colleagues, is committed to devoting time to its development and success. Their business alliance is built upon a bedrock of solid friendship, which they consider will be one of its major strengths. Said Sean Pertwee, 'It gives us a tremendous sense of stability and self-confidence.' The equity extends to all the actors having equal shares in Natural Nylon, along with their two producers Damon Bryant and Bradley Adams – the latter of whom stated that a significant reason for forming the production company was to allow actors like McGregor the chance to garner experience in the crucial behind-the-scenes decision-making stages of movies. 'This company gives him the mechanism to develop a product that he likes.'

In film-making terms there has never been any secret about what McGregor likes. 'We've got really good writers here [in Britain]. We've got incredible facilities and all the studios are brilliant. We've got the best technicians in the world and we make terribly good movies. They're not gonna make $400 million – but then they're not going to cost $400 million either.' Adding, 'The quality of our work is also far superior.' He also pulls no punches when it comes to his view of LA. 'It's just a town about the movies. So it's kind of just movies made about other movies. In Britain we can make movies about people and the way we live our lives and that's what interests me more.'

The reaction to the Natural Nylon initiative from within the film world is one of genuine encouragement. Director Carl Prechezer, with whom McGregor worked in his early days on the film *Blue Juice*, applauded this move to set up a new production company. 'It's an incredible time just now, with a level of funding that we haven't seen for years, which provides so many opportunities. Actors mature faster in this kind of climate than they did, say, ten years ago. And they don't wait for plum roles to come along. Instead, they generate them.'

Film critic Barry Norman says, 'It depends what their aim is. If they want to make a *Titanic* – forget it. They'd never get the money. But if they are interested in making British films – and not just with British themes and casts, but also financed here too – then that can only be very healthy for the industry and the best of luck to them. The great tragedy of *The Full Monty* was that it was financed by Twentieth Century Fox and all the profits went to America. It wasn't that the makers of *The Full Monty* wanted it that way, but Fox were the only ones to come in with a decent offer. If Natural Nylon can avoid that kind of thing, then it will be great.'

Lord David Puttnam calls it, 'An admirable ambition' to take on the might of Hollywood. Time and again it is stated that the biggest problem with British films is the number that never make it to the cinema circuit. But according to Puttnam, 'Distribution is not the real problem. Cinemas are run as self-sustaining businesses. They are not going to show films that won't bring in money. Blaming the distribution side of things is something of a created myth these days. It is marketing that is important – the PR behind a film, having the confidence that it should be a big hit and ploughing money into promotion.'

He goes on, '*Brassed Off* did well and was successful, but *The Full Monty* was the one nominated for Oscars and its makers were clever. It opened first in America, just as *Four Weddings and a Funeral* did, and the UK media picked up on the success of the relatively small British movie in the States, so that they then brought it in to this country as an already established success. It says something dreadful about the British media. *That* is the serious problem. The British press won't take a chance on a film unless its popularity has safely been proved elsewhere.'

Having an instinct for which are the best films to make will also enter the equation when it comes to ascertaining whether Natural Nylon will prove to be a long-term success. Their first batch of potential projects, revealed in December 1997, was said to include a historical drama called *The Hellfire Club* in which all five actors are tipped to star. Based upon the infamous antics of a select circle of eighteenth-century aristocratic rakes and libertines, notorious for their excessive drunken and promiscuous pursuits, it will definitely not conform to the traditional costume-drama format. Says Sadie Frost, 'This is going to be dark and dirty – a bit edgy.' Shooting for this is projected to start around August 1999, the first available time when all five individuals will be free of other commitments.

A number of other projects are in the pipeline. Jude Law was said to be lining up a role as the poet Christopher Marlowe in a period comedy, *Marlowe*, to be directed by Iain Softley, said to be scheduled to start production in summer 1998. Softley was also said to be due, straight after this, at the helm of a mystical thriller called *The Boathouse* starring Milla Jovovich. A biopic of the late Brian Epstein, the Beatles manager who died tragically young in 1967, has also been mentioned, as has a film version of Christopher Fowler's grim horror novel *Psychoville*. It had also been suggested that Ewan McGregor would star as James Joyce in a film about the writer's wife Nora Barnacle. A couple of other projects were floated as possibilities, including one co-production, *eXistenZ* – a film which would have special significance for McGregor.

Through Natural Nylon McGregor, it was revealed, would be making his first foray into the role of film producer. *eXistenZ*, a science fiction thriller, was to be made in cooperation with one of Natural Nylon's backers Alliance Pictures. It tells the futuristic story of a world in which computer game designers are the new royalty. One designer of virtual reality games creates a game that blurs the edges between reality and make-believe and in the process comes under threat from murderous fans.

Shooting started on this $23 million movie on 6 April 1998 in Toronto, starring Jennifer Jason Leigh, Jude Law, Willem Dafoe and Ian Holm. It is directed by David Cronenberg, with McGregor in the producer's hotseat.

It all made for an exciting and varied path ahead. But when filming had ended on *Rogue Trader* McGregor did manage to fit in a month's break; he needed to be with his family to unwind. He had to step back into the acting spotlight in February 1998 to attend the UK premiere, in Glasgow, of *The Serpent's Kiss*. His appearance, wife-swapping jokes aside, allowed him to bring a moment of happiness to a long-standing film buff.

Bob Stewart from Bearsden in Glasgow is the chief projectionist at Greenock's Waterfront cinema which is managed by his wife Mary. Between them they have racked up seventy-five years in the business; moreover, Bob has in the last six years, in support of Glasgow Film Theatre's seat sponsorship scheme, dedicated fifteen seats to various stars of the silver screen. McGregor is the honorary patron of this scheme which was set up to give serious film lovers the vehicle to raise much-needed money for cinemas.

The former patron had been none other than the US superstar Robert De Niro. He had been moved to head this fundraising scheme in 1992 when he learned that the first seat Bob Stewart had sponsored had been in his name: a delighted De Niro had written a personal letter to Bob. McGregor also had a surprise for him – as Bob explains. 'On the Sunday night I got a call from the woman who runs the Glasgow Film Theatre seat sponsorship scheme asking if I and my wife were coming to a semi-nar the following week. She said, "Ewan McGregor and Denis Lawson will be there." I said I didn't know. I might be working.' He goes on, 'Nearer the time she rang me again and that time I said, "Och aye, then. It'll pass the time." Only when I got there I was told they were going to give me a certificate for all the work I've done on the scheme over the years, and that Ewan McGregor was going to present it to me.'

The surprise could hardly have been greater. As Bob recalls, 'It was nerve-racking accepting the certificate in front of a packed cinema full of 400 people.' He was really impressed with how down-to-earth McGregor was. 'We had a chat in the bar afterwards,' says Bob. 'And he's really a very nice young man – very friendly. I've been forty-three years in the business and I liked his attitude. I told Ewan and Denis Lawson that the very next seat I am going to sponsor will be for them and Ewan was thrilled.'

Come the start of March 1998 McGregor's family break had ended and work took over once again. Just as the trade newspaper *The Hollywood Reporter* issued their list of The Most Bankable Stars, which included McGregor in the 'Shooting Stars' category, he was recalled to Leavesden Studios in Hertfordshire for three weeks of reshoots for *Star Wars*. The work in question centred around vital scenes between Obi-Wan Kenobi and the ancient Jedi master, Yoda.

Following this McGregor went straight to Montreal in Canada to com-mence work on his latest film, a $15 million American independent psy-chological crime story called *Eye Of The Beholder*. It was to be a remake of a low-key original French version: the erotic script based on the steamy novel by Marc Behm had been completed and was to be directed by Australian Stephan Elliott, whose previous films included the cheerfully vulgar 1994 comedy-musical *The Adventures Of Priscilla, Queen Of The Desert*. This movie would be very different. A complex tale, it involves a bizarre love story and features a private detective (McGregor) who has been tracking a female serial killer across the United States for over ten years. Convinced of her innocence, he is certain that she needs his help. The serial killer, Joanna, is played by American actress Ashley Judd, previ-ously featured in the controversial Warner Brothers film *Natural Born Killers* as well as Joel Schumacher's drama *A Time To Kill*.

'There are a great many good independent movies coming out of America,' said McGregor. 'I'm really interested in making movies like that.' Relishing this new and quirky role, he knuckled down under Stephan Elliott's direction – only to find the entire experience particularly gruelling in the brief time schedule allowed. 'It almost put me in the grave,' he later recalled. 'It's a really well thought-out movie, but tough. When I came off *Eye Of The Beholder* I was really on the edge of losing my mind.'

Before he could reach such a crisis point, as a proud Scot work and career were temporarily suspended when the second week of June arrived. It was the start of the 1998 football World Cup hosted by France, and McGregor took time off from filming *Eye Of The Beholder* to make his way to Paris in anticipation of an historic occasion: the Scotland national football squad facing the mighty Cup holders Brazil in the opening match at the Stade de France in Paris on Wednesday 10 June.

It was to be a family holiday, with his parents and brother also joining him. For a couple of days before the match he frequented pubs like The Auld Alliance, a replica of an Edinburgh bar in Paris, to soak up the electric atmosphere generated by the hordes of the famous Tartan Army – the thousands-strong vocal but friendly travelling Scottish football fan clan – clad in kilts, draped in Scottish Lion Rampart flags, with painted faces and blaring the bagpipes. Photographed in the Press hugely enjoying himself with some of these rollicking good-natured supporters, McGregor melted naturally into their ranks, even phoning home to Scotland on behalf of some of the men to pass on their loved ones' messages that they were having a great, but safe, time.

On the eve of the big game nerves were taut when McGregor joined television personality Ulrika Jonsson, English sports commentator Jimmy Hill and actor Richard Wilson on the *McCoist and MacAulay BBC 1 World Cup Special* live from a studio set up inside the Eiffel Tower. Marching on set through the studio audience, unshaven and wearing a kilt of the McGregor tartan and a Scotland football top, he suddenly took a run at the stage and lobbed a plastic bottle at the huge glass window behind the sofas (naturally it bounced harmlessly off) – picking up on an earlier challenge from one of the presenters for someone to break the window to prove the programme really *was* being broadcast live from inside France's most famous landmark.

Somewhat disappointed with his pre-match prediction of either a 3–2 win or a draw for his team – Scotland went down 2–1 – the partying nevertheless continued and McGregor boozed well into the night at the £100-a-head bash at the exclusive Buddha Bar in Paris amongst a merry band of Scottish celebrities, including soccer legend Kenny Dalglish, footballer Ally McCoist, former Formula One world motor-racing champion Jackie Stewart and superstar Sean Connery, all awash with fervent patriotism.

Before Scotland's next game, however, McGregor had to leave. 'It's my first trip abroad to watch Scotland play and I've had such a fantastic time,' he revealed. 'I'd love to have gone on to Bordeaux but I don't have the time.' He added, 'Of course, if we make it to the final I'll be back in Paris for a beer with the lads.' Buoyed up by this ill-founded optimism he jetted back to Canada to finish filming his final scenes for *Eye Of The Beholder*, the expected release date for which is thought to be early in 1999.

Just as McGregor had missed a *Velvet Goldmine* pre-launch party in London in mid-December 1997 due to the filming of *Rogue Trader*, so his commitments in Canada now prevented him from joining director Todd Haynes and the rest of the cast of the glam-rock film when it premiered at the 1998 Cannes Film Festival in May. It was whilst reporting from the French Riviera that *Daily Mail* showbiz columnist Baz Bamigboye revealed what he termed a scoop: that the Scottish actor was ready to take on the lead in 1998/99 in a film version by Roger Michell of the Louis de Bernières bestselling novel *Captain Corelli's Mandolin*. The eponymous captain, based on the Greek Island of Cephalonia during its Italian-German occupation, becomes entangled in a love triangle with the spirited Pelagina and the local man to whom she is promised in marriage.

It had also been established that McGregor was definitely to star as James Joyce in Natural Nylon's film project *Nora*. Following Stephen Fry's acclaimed portrayal of Oscar Wilde in the Brian Gilbert-directed historial drama *Wilde*, interest in Irish writers had intensified and there was speculation that Daniel Day-Lewis had been tipped to play Samuel Beckett in a biopic project by *My Left Foot* producer Noel Pearson. *Nora*, then, would be in keeping with this trend.

James Augustine Aloysius Joyce was born in Dublin in 1882 and educated at the city's University College. At the age of twenty-one he went
to study medicine in Paris, ended up living the life of a starving would-
be poet. After failing to support himself as a writer back in Ireland, he
journeyed to Trieste with Nora Barnacle, his wife and constant companion, to teach English. He eventually landed in Zurich with Nora and
formed a company of Irish theatre players before again settling in Paris.
He died in 1941.

The film *Nora*, in which actress Susan Lynch will play Joyce's wife, is to
be directed and written by Pat Murphy; and is scheduled to start shooting around March 1999. For McGregor it would mark his second biopic.
As always McGregor had been doing his homework, researching the role
by becoming a regular visitor to the James Joyce Centre in Dublin.
However, not everyone, even at this early pre-shooting stage, seemed convinced that he was suited to the part. James Joyce's nephew Ken
Monaghan was reported to have commented, on McGregor's casting, 'I
don't know how he's going to do it, because he's a lot shorter than Joyce.'

Starring as the celebrated Irish writer would move McGregor yet again
into new and challenging territory in a world in which his acting stature,
already high, was only on the increase. And as autumn 1998 approached
he was about to take yet another unexpected and brave step.

CHAPTER 12

Feel The Force

EXPANDING HIS REPERTOIRE has always been something at which McGregor excels – although, despite his skill at singing and dancing, it is extremely unlikely that he will ever be seen in a stage musical. 'It's not something I'm very interested in,' he says. 'In London, musicals have taken over the West End in such a huge way that there's not much room left for a straight play any more and that's a shame.' However, he clearly still hankers after the immediacy of stage work. For Press speculation which began in February 1998 surrounding the possibility that Ewan McGregor might make his major London stage debut in the autumn was confirmed in the summer by McGregor himself when he revealed that he would be appearing in a north London theatre in November.

He would be following the latest vogue among some of the acting world's biggest stars who were making surprise sorties into theatreland. The Australian-born Hollywood actress Nicole Kidman, wife of heart-throb actor Tom Cruise and star of such movies as the screen adaptation of Henry James, *Portrait Of A Lady* and Stanley Kubrick's *Eyes Wide Shut*, had likewise decided to tread the boards in September at Covent Garden's Donmar Warehouse in David Hare's *The Blue Room*, an adaptation of Arthur Schnitzler's sensual play *La Ronde*.

McGregor was to step off the film-making treadmill to star as Malcolm Scrawdyke, the rebellious loudmouth in the Sixties play *Little Malcolm And His Struggle Against The Eunuchs*. Written by David Halliwell, the story portrays a bunch of art students who turn bolshie when the college authorities appear to be restricting their freedom of expression.

The play, opening on 12 November, was to run initially until 12 January 1999 at the Hampstead Theatre Club at the Swiss Cottage Centre very convenient, as McGregor was staying nearby in Belsize Park. Co-starring Joe Duttine, Sean Gilder and Nicolas Tennant, the play would mark McGregor's first professional working association with his uncle: Denis Lawson was to be the play's director. 'I begged him to direct it,' said McGregor, explaining that he had opted for this 'mammoth' part because he felt it would stretch him. 'I haven't been on a stage for some time so I wanted a fright,' he declared.

He went on, 'I made the decision when I was working in Utah on *A Life Less Ordinary*. I phoned Denis, who has always been someone I can moan to when I need to. I said I would only do a play if he would agree to direct, because it's such a terrifying prospect.' Still, as the five weeks of rehearsal approached he found that he had been right to make this decision. 'I felt a need to do it because I miss the intensity of rehearsals. I am tired of being asked to do emotionally risky things in front of a camera without having been given a second to get there myself. There is no respect in the movies for creative talent. In the theatre, people understand your needs.'

It went without saying that he was certain Denis Lawson in his capacity as director would see and understand his needs – but as to whether their being related would cause any professional awkwardness McGregor, who continues to credit Lawson with having been a rock upon which he had leant in his early acting days, made a good-natured threat. 'If he gives me a bad call, I will call him "Uncle Denis". ' And there was to be another familiar connection in the shape of one of the play's co-stars, Lou Gish, whose actress mother Sheila Gish is Denis Lawson's longtime partner.

In advance of the play's opening night Ewan anticipated little kindness from the theatrical press. 'People are going to slag me off, but I couldn't give a fuck. Theatre critics will want to hammer me.' The reasoning behind this prediction soon became clear. 'There is far too much infighting between the theatre and the film industry. Both disciplines can learn from each other. It's crazy to have this looking-down-your-nose-at-each-other attitude.'

The public's reaction, however, quickly proved to be nothing but positive and the play sold out in advance of opening night. It was reported

RIGHT Pictured with actress Brenda Blethyn at an awards ceremony. The pair worked well alongside Jane Horrocks and Michael Caine in the sensational hit movie *Little Voice*.

BELOW Sunning himself with Anna Friel on the Singapore set of *Rogue Trader*, the 1999 biopic of Nick Leeson.

Ewan McGregor, a proud Scot, takes every opportunity to wear his country's national dress.

later that McGregor had personally helped cope with demand by manning the telephone lines at the booking office; and that on the black market, at one point, a £16 ticket was fetching somewhere in the region of £250. The 174-seat Hampstead Theatre with its intimate setting – the stage is the same size as the seating area – is run as a club whose clientele is normally drawn from the more mature theatregoing set but the rush for tickets as soon as Ewan McGregor's involvement was announced was such that the theatre's financial manager, Christopher Beard, revealed that young girls were joining the club purely in order to be able to see the play. He also voiced a collective concern: that McGregor's female admirers might prove so excitable and noisy that they would stop Ewan remembering his lines.

Those fears were to prove groundless. From its opening night *Little Malcolm* became a huge success; despite McGregor's previous predictions his performance drew glowing reviews. Certainly some guest reviewers on the BBC 2 TV show *Late Review* commented that Ewan was too charming to be completely convincing as an evil bully, and also that the production at times resembled an end-of-term play with McGregor indulging himself in a bit of fun. But the film critic of the *Daily Mail* trumpeted his performance as 'superb', a magnificent triumph, adding, 'Bearded, clad in a black greatcoat and gimlet-eyed, McGregor makes a most sympathetic, charismatic lout. He struts and harangues like a tin-pot tyrant, but shrivels and stutters at the thought of confronting the girl he fancies.' And elsewhere the praise also flowed lavishly.

From the start McGregor himself took a low-key approach. There was no 'luvvie' first night party, instead he went with his parents and Denis Lawson for a meal. And even when the plaudits flooded in he remained level-headed and steadfastly democratic about it all. When the play's run began in November 1998 the cast were all on the Equity minimum rate of pay for an 'off-West End' theatre production of £250 a week. Because of the play's popularity, however, by early December it was reported that its run was going to be extended by a further eight weeks; moreover it was moving to the more mainstream, much larger Comedy Theatre in the West End. A film star of McGregor's standing could reasonably expect to command a substantial wage in addition to receiving a percentage of the ticket sales, and indeed at this juncture it was said that Ewan had been offered a weekly pay packet of £10,000. But he had turned this down, preferring that an 'ensemble deal' be struck: one that meant his four co-stars were paid the same as himself – £900 a week and an equal share of any profits.

That McGregor would see-saw quite so dramatically in his choice of work projects – and be so fair-minded at the same time – appealed to fellow actors. Says Isla Blair, 'This is what is great about him. He'll do *Star Wars* and he'll do Hampstead Theatre for something like a couple of hundred pounds a week.' Besides the fact that money was not a consideration, and that he would be working alongside the source of his original inspiration, McGregor, who had done very little theatre work, was actively looking forward to the challenge, even under what would surely be a bright spotlight.

Speaking of his first return to the stage since appearing at Salisbury Playhouse in the Sixties farce *What The Butler Saw* five hectic years before, he said, 'It's completely different work. It's the same thing – you're just pretending to be someone else. But with movies you're just capturing moments. So every day you maybe capture five or six moments in say thirty or forty seconds. Whereas on stage you can get a run at it and it's more of a challenge creatively.'

When the play's run was over it was rumoured that his working association with his uncle might not be at an end. McGregor's and Lawson's names had been linked with a film about the thorny question of Scottish devolution. Called *Don't Think Twice* – a twist on the 'Think Twice' campaign slogan of the anti-devolutionists – apparently the film was going to be shot around the Scottish west coast town of Oban.

The range of projects touted as possibly starring McGregor (in addition to *Captain Corelli's Mandolin* and *Nora*) numbered five, with no less than four of them being biopics. He was said to be in a shortlist alongside Colin Firth to portray the dark and brooding fictional hero Heathcliffe in a proposed two-hour LWT film version of Emily Bronte's classic *Wuthering Heights* – the romantic period tale of love and obsession last filmed in 1993 with Ralph Fiennes as the possessive and windswept lover.

In December 1997 film-makers were openly hoping to pair him with Sean Connery in a movie charting the life of Thomas Blake Glover, who was born in the north-east Scottish coastal town of Fraserburgh in the nineteenth century. He went to live and work in Japan as a shipping clerk and became so phenomenally successful a trader that he is credited with kickstarting the industrial revolution in the land of the Rising Sun. Written by Alan Spence, the film's producer Sir Richard Scott-Thompson envisages McGregor portraying Glover as a young man, with Connery taking over as he gets older. It might not be a forlorn hope on Scott-Thompson's part; McGregor has publicly said, 'If there isn't anything involving Sean Connery, then we'll have to arrange it.' He was also mentioned as being under consideration for the role of Scots poet and ladies man Robert Burns, in a planned movie of his literary career and womanising exploits: a part with which Jonny Lee Miller's name was also being connected.

Scottish roles aside, just prior to reports of the Thomas Blake Glover part the *Times* cited McGregor as 'likely' to be cast as Samuel Taylor Coleridge in a £4 million BBC feature film about the Romantic poet William Wordsworth and his friendship and collaboration with Coleridge. Based on a screenplay by Frank Cottrell Boyce and produced by Michael Kustow, this controversial film is thought to depict Wordsworth as a bully and argues that he betrayed Coleridge and helped push him towards a drug addition that almost cost Coleridge his life. Said to be scheduled for shooting some time in 1999, its director is Julien Temple who directed the 1980 film about the Sex Pistols, *The Great Rock And Roll Swindle*.

And it was in the world of rock music that the last of these four projected biopics was set. McGregor's name was being squeezed firmly into the frame as the man tipped to portray rock legend John Lennon, who was cold-bloodedly gunned down by deranged fan Mark Chapman outside his apartment in New York City late at night on 8 December 1980. The *Times* released news that a £40 million Hollywood movie from Columbia Pictures was being planned; the film company's president, Amy Pascal, was said to have eventually persuaded Yoko Ono to tell her's and Lennon's story in her own way.

In addition to charting the development of Lennon's love for Ono after his marriage to wife Cynthia failed, the film had the potential to be controversial: it would depict Yoko Ono as someone who eased friction between John and songwriting partner Paul McCartney rather than attempting to sever the relationship. It was even suggested that the film would seek to reveal a radically new picture of Ono struggling single-handedly to prevent the Beatles from imploding towards the end of the Sixties – a portrayal that would contradict much that has been said about the Beatles. Paul McCartney was reported as keeping his eye on these Hollywood machinations with 'interest'.

Four months later, on 28 December, the *Sunday Times*, reporting on this planned movie, unequivocally quoted it as 'starring Ewan McGregor'. And elsewhere Yoko Ono, who was said to be taking a keen interest in the casting of all the Beatles' members, was allegedly happy with McGregor as the choice for Lennon. But, if anything *had* been decided, there appeared to be some uncertainty in McGregor's mind. When asked about the project he replied, 'I think it would be a dodgy thing to do, just politically, in terms of the other band members and stuff, because they're all well against it, aren't they? Paul McCartney and Co.'

Whether McGregor would appear in any or all of these projects, come spring 1999 all eyes were firmly glued on the release, on 21 May, of *Star Wars Episode I*. The anticipation had been building for some considerable time amid speculation, fuelled by the intense secrecy surrounding the film, as to what it would be like and how it would measure up to the much-loved originals. Prequels, like sequels, can be notoriously tricky. In this case there was the added dimension that *Episodes I-III* were said to alter all currently held perceptions of *Episodes IV-VI*. George Lucas had warned, 'It's going to change the first three movies rather dramatically.' He said that that was his major reason for resuscitating the space saga; he had enjoyed, he said, having the chance to take something long established as one thing and put a new spin on it. McGregor, viewing the overall project says, 'There's eighteen months of post-production. There was two years of pre-production and three and a half months of shooting. That shows you how important the acting is. I think I did a good job and the film will turn out to be absolutely what it was meant to be.'

Terence Stamp, as the President of the Galaxy in *Episode I*, did not sign a secrecy agreement; as he revealed of actors like himself who were given cameo roles, 'We weren't given a full script. I was just given my few pages.' He said, after filming his scenes in 1997, 'When I finished my part and it was time to leave the set, I knew the others were going to do another three months and I was really jealous. I just wanted to be in for the whole trip. It was a *very* good feeling on the set. I was with Ewan McGregor, Liam Neeson and a heavenly girl Natalie Portman – a really amazing cinema animal. I have a feeling it's going to be extraordinary.'

All whispers did indeed point to it being a tremendous treat in store. Lucas stoked the rampant anticipation when asked about the possibility of a trailer appearing: 'It will probably be in December 1998.' Prior to this though there emerged, as summer 1998 wore on, a raft of unsubstantiated rumours that the production was in some difficulty. Stories circulated that, because of blue tinges on the faces of some of the actors in some scenes, whole chunks of the movie would need to be reshot. Reassuringly, however, by September the film's producer Rick McCallum went on record to report, 'ILM are doing the most phenomenal job. The quality is so extremely good that it is mind-boggling.' It was a sentiment which dovetailed exactly with other news reported around this time – that George Lucas had invited director Steven Spielberg privately to see some rough cuts of the new *Star Wars* and that the Oscar-winning Spielberg had been so blown away by what he had seen that he publicly predicted of the film, 'It'll make your jaw hang out for a week!'

McGregor had found the blue-screen acting a disconcerting experience but his excitement about the finished product was tangible. 'The best thing, the really weird thing, will be eventually seeing it once all the effects have been added in,' he said, ' 'cos we won't have seen any of that. It'll be like seeing yourself in a dream. Can you imagine what it'll be like sitting down in some screening room, the curtain going up – and there it is the new *Star Wars* movie! Magic!'

This degree of unabashed enthusiasm is typical of his positive, go-getter attitude to life; in some ways it can be attributed to the charmed path it has taken. Following a secure and happy upbringing he quickly entered into a blissful marriage which equally quickly produced a daughter whom he cherishes. Being a husband and a father at an age and stage in his career when he could have been footloose and free only thrills him. He does not care that there are those who find his uxoriousness unusual. 'We're happy. We can travel around together and all I know is it's so good to have them with me.' It is typical too of McGregor's luck that his married state manages in no way to dent his pull as a screen heart-throb.

The tranquility of his marriage though, had not always remained undis-turbed, as in September 1998 McGregor was prepared to reveal. According to him the reasons were two-fold. In the first instance the pres-sure of his incessant workload had taken its toll, and this was coupled to the lasting effects of the scare he and his wife Eve had suffered over their daughter's health the year before.

'It's quite a strain on many relationships when you are denied space and time together,' he confessed. 'I had no time and I wasn't seeing my wife properly, or my daughter. I'd been going straight from one film to the next for three years, which is the best situation for an actor to be in, but it was breaking my back. I was losing it. Dealing with success is quite difficult. You're meant to enjoy the whole process. It's a bit like what being pregnant is for a woman. It's meant to be all rosy and you're not meant to complain, so you keep it all inside, which can be hard.'

Denis Lawson had been aware of these pressures on McGregor. 'Ewan went through several years of finishing a movie on one night at 7.00 pm and at 6.00 am being on another set. He's a very strong guy – but that's too stressful.'

It was also still hard on Ewan to remember that he had been away, ful-filling contractual work obligations, when Clara had fallen ill. 'My daugh-ter almost died and I wasn't there to help,' he recalled; although he had dropped everything and flown home as soon as he heard the news, he admitted that, when Clara eventually pulled through, he and Eve were again denied the chance, because of work, to recover together from the stress they had undergone.

'Eve dealt with it on her own and so did I, which was a mistake. We should have done it together,' he stated. 'You can't just breeze through those kinds of things. There are a lot of feelings that have to be thrashed out afterwards.' He added, 'We have had a lot of talking to do over the last summer. Now I just want more time with Eve to make it better.'

Professionally too, until autumn 1998, he had been nothing but happy – such had been the amazing meteroric trajectory of his career. 'I never thought I was special,' he said. 'I just felt truly that this was something I should be doing.' Not one given to too much philosophising, he none the less firmly believes that, although nothing guarantees happiness, it does helps to identify what it is that drives you: something he recognised as a young boy of nine. 'I do think it's to do with finding what makes you who you are,' he maintained. Being an actor does it for him.

It was inevitable though that a point would arrive when the brakes would have to be temporarily applied to such a frantic schedule. The trick was in recognising that point, which McGregor did at about the same time as he realised that he needed to retrench as far as his family was concerned. 'I am just exhausted,' he admitted as autumn 1998 approached. 'I have become tainted with the whole thing. I've pushed my career as far as I could in a short space of time, but it has become totally mad.' His reaction was to postpone making any more films until early 1999.

The plan to enjoy a hassle-free couple of months, however, was interrupted by a series of minor hitches. It started off peacefully enough when, in mid-August, he returned to his home town to help launch the annual Crieff Highland Games. The Press were on hand to capture a bearded McGregor falling short on brawn when it came to trying to lift and toss the caber – a twenty-foot solid wooden pole. Giving up after several attempts he joked that he might stand a chance if the pole was cut in half. But three days later it was the managing director of St Johnstone football club who was doing the tossing, in a manner of speaking, when Stewart Duff asked Ewan to leave the Campbell Suite, the executive lounge at the club's ground, McDiarmid Park.

McGregor had arrived at the lounge to team up with his friend, striker Ally McCoist, who had debuted for the visiting team Kilmarnock that day. He was there simply to enjoy a relaxing drink with McCoist, but a member complained that the actor's casual jeans and T-shirt contravened the club's strict dress code. When Stewart Duff asked the young star to leave McGregor did so, completely unfazed. 'I didn't have a tie on. It was fair enough,' he later shrugged.

By the following month, after he had stepped off the treadmill to spend more time with his wife and child, he attended the Deauville Film Festival in France, where a storm in a teacup temporarily erupted. A French colleague had asked McGregor about Scotland's most famous actor Sean Connery and Ewan's unguarded reply quickly found its way into the Press. Scotland's biggest-selling tabloid newspaper, the *Daily Record* emblazoned a story of a full-blooded feud between the two Scots stars on its front page on 17 September.

McGregor's comments were said to have emanated from the time, earlier in the year during the World Cup, when Scottish celebrities had thronged into Paris's exclusive Buddha Bar. A picture emerged of that night which suggested McGregor had wanted to meet the legendary Connery but had been too shy to approach him in person. Ewan's brother Colin had paved the way and at first McGregor had enjoyed the former 007 actor's company. As the night wore on, however – at least, so it was reported by journalists present – Connery's fervent passion for the Scottish Nationalist Party and their call for Scottish independence grew to a pitch that many present found to be intense.

McGregor's remarks to the French colleague at the Deauville Film Festival were typically uncompromising. 'I don't like to be told by anyone how to feel about being Scottish. Nobody has the right to tell me – especially somebody who hasn't lived there for twenty-five years!' Interestingly, the result of a telephone poll which the *Daily Record* set up which invited readers to vote according to whether they supported Connery's stand or McGregor's, came out in McGregor's favour: fifty-three per cent voted for the younger star, with the remainder voting for Connery. McGregor was clearly uncomfortable with all the fuss and within days he completely distanced himself from it all, saying that he felt his comments about Connery were 'perhaps inappropriate'. 'I love his acting and I never had a fight with him. Complete nonsense. My beliefs have always been my own,' he said, 'but it's embarrassing to be held up as some kind of figurehead in the independence debate.'

The matter vanished as quickly as it had flared. McGregor, however, flew literally straight into another drama, this time of the real-life sort when, at the end of September, he went to join comedian Lenny Henry in Cape Town to film a scene for an upcoming Comic Relief documentary. The incident happened when the helicopter that McGregor was travelling in was mistaken by South African guards for an enemy gunship. When the craft landed it was immediately surrounded and searched by armed guards, who suspected its occupants of being on the way to Lesotho to assist the rebels engaged in fighting with the South African border troops. All ended well – but it must have been a hairy few moments.

Through all this, in his propulsion to international fame and pin-up status, McGregor has managed to stay refreshingly normal. He has carried out many a magazine photo session, but posing and being pampered do not appeal to him. Nor is he interested in being a fashion plate. 'I'm not trendy at all,' he admitted. 'Most of my nice clothes I've got from films I've been in.'

He does like to indulge his penchant for motorbikes, however, and has become involved with a superbike racing team called GenerRace which is made up of jobbing actors, technicians and so on. He had been told about this by actor Charlie Boorman on the set of *The Serpent's Kiss*: Boorman later said 'Ewan has been great giving us so much time, as he is so busy.' But McGregor needs little encouragement to straddle one of the powerful machines. His interest in them began when he was fourteen but his mother put her foot down and it was not until he landed in London that he acquired his first bike. Today he favours a distinctive canary yellow Ducati 748 SP. 'Motorbikes are my passion. Riding them singles your mind. That's why people climb mountains. I love speed, going round lovely curvy corners. I feel a great disturbance in my leather trousers when riding fast,' he declares.

As a workaholic actor he remains uninhibited and indiscreet – he can display an often shocking candour at times about his own profession. Directors, producers, writers and fellow actors will line up to attest to just how 'ordinary' he has remained; although the biggest test of this will come after the release of *Star Wars Episode I*. He certainly feels the weight of expectation.

'Everyone's constantly been trying to scare me about what my life's going to turn into,' he reveals. 'It's something that's out of your control anyway. Also I don't worry myself with that side of things. In my life it was another job. Of course, it was a huge job, because it's *Star Wars*. But there's nothing I would do to prepare myself for what might happen. If that had been a concern, you'd have to think twice about doing the film. It wasn't.'

The prospect of even more intense media and Press interest in her husband is something about which Eve Mavrakis has made her views plain. 'Ewan is very close to his family. I am very close to my family. We have the same values. But it is quite pernicious, they way it hits you. The papers always say, "Oh, Ewan, he's so nice, so grounded," but Ewan is a nice guy, so even if he's not grounded, he's going to be nice. It's more pernicious the way it comes in. It has other ways to touch people and to hurt them. I'm not sure of it yet. I'm still watching.'

As to how hard it will be for McGregor to resist the seductive beam of Hollywood, Lord David Puttnam says, 'It comes down to a test of character. Intelligence and strength of character is what is needed and I have every confidence in Ewan. He is a solid, smart guy and not at all silly. You create what you do. It's a question of what is important to you – being able to go out and make the big bucks in an American movie, then make a smaller British film. It's all about finding the balance and asking yourself, "Do you see yourself as a person entitled to a life, or a commodity?" '

And Barry Norman believes, 'He is a level-headed young man with his feet firmly on the ground. Big screen success will come with *Star Wars* and the offers will flood in, I'm sure. It depends on what he does. It depends on what he goes for – the money, or the role? So far, he has gone for the role and it is to his credit. It's down to him choosing his roles and why. Of course, he could have the best of both worlds. He could make the big American movies which will enhance his international standing *and* make the smaller films which will develop his scope as an actor. For an actor, that's an ideal life and I'm sure it could be his. The temptations will be great, though.'

They could scarcely come greater than *Star Wars* being hailed as 'the movie event of the millennium'. When asked how he personally responded to this pressure, George Lucas replied, 'The fact that everybody goes crazy for it is fine – but I'm just telling a story I want to tell. It's like a symphony more than a movie.'

Certainly the sound of cash tills ringing will be music to the film backers' ears; *Star Wars Episode I* is expected to shatter box-office records around the world when it explodes onto the scene in May 1999. And the commercial spin-offs will be staggering, further fuelling the movie mania and burning the faces of the film's stars ever deeper into the collective consciousness. McGregor's image as Obi-Wan Kenobi will be brandished far and wide on clothes, board and computer games, on cereal boxes, duvet covers and wall hangings, lunchboxes and magazine front covers. Several corporations have already made sure of that.

In 1996 – three years before the film's release – the soft drinks giant Pepsi won, in a massive bidding exercise, contracts that will mean that

Ewan McGregor's face will be wrapped around cans of cola. For this privilege Pepsi paid sweet – $2 billion. And whilst filming was underway in 1997 another bidding frenzy erupted among America's biggest toy manufacturers for the rights to make the next range of *Star Wars* toys – they too were talking telephone numbers. The licences were to be awarded by George Lucas: Mattel, the makers of the Barbie doll, was just one of the companies weighing in, in their case with a bid of $1 billion for a ten-year package. But Lucas chose to stick with Hasbro Inc and Galoob Toys Inc, the original makers of the *Star Wars* toys whose licensing deal ran out in 1998.

Twentieth Century Fox secured the distribution rights to all three prequels in April 1998. Fox CEO Peter Chernin said, 'There is so much risk associated with "tentpole" films. We have the incredible luxury of knowing that over three summers we have *the* event movie of the summer.' By January 1999 movie insiders were predicting that *Star Wars Episode I: The Phantom Menace* with its £80 million of special effects would obliterate *Titanic's* record $1 billion box-office receipts by raking in this astronomical earnings over its opening weekend alone. A Fox executive was quoted as saying, 'The movie is still being edited and the publicity campaign has already started. It's the first time George has directed since *Star Wars* and he's adamant he will top the first three films, and show James Cameron exactly who's the boss of Hollywood.'

It looked like a safe prediction, too, when on 17 November a two-minute trailer for *Star Wars Episode I*, screened in seventy-five selected cinemas across America, provoked an unprecedented public reaction. The brief trailer was being shown with either the new Bruce Willis action movie *The Siege* or Brad Pitt's *Meet Joe Black*, and crowds of people were cramming into the cinemas simply to see the trailer then leaving before the main feature had started. Tickets began changing hands for ten times their face value; yet even so, in one New York cinema alone nearly 500 punters left after seeing the trailer for the first time only to queue outside the same cinema for close on three hours to see it again at the next showing.

There was an unprecedented rush reported when it emerged that over four million people logged on to the website within half an hour of *Star Wars* information appearing on the Internet. The excited clamour to see the trailer set America alight; even on the basis of only a small teaser of the movie, people of all ages were completely blown away. McGregor, his hair swept dashingly back, in full flight wielding his lightsaber or piloting an escaping spacecraft, came in for particular praise as the anticipation reached stratospheric proportions for the release of this same two-minute trailer on British cinema screens. Prior to its UK premiere at London's Odeon in Leicester Square on 16 December it was being widely reported that hordes were expected to file into the theatre to catch a glimpse of things to come; reports which were borne out when hundreds packed into the Odeon, only to burst into spontaneous applause at the end of the brief showing. The trailer gave little of the still closely guarded plot away, but this failed to diminish interest in the taster when it went on general release throughout Britain two days later.

Principal photography is scheduled to commence on *Episode II* the year following *Episode I*'s release. McGregor revealed, 'We start filming the sequel in January 2000. There's rumours they might film *II* and *III* back to back. Nobody knows what's going on except George Lucas, and he's not telling anyone anything.' The story for these two films is still in development but the subtitles to *Episodes II* and *III* are said to be, respectively, *Rise Of The Empire* and *Fall Of The Jedi*. In January 1999 George Lucas confirmed rumours that his company would be shooting *Episode II* in Australia, with work taking place at the Fox Studios in Sydney. Post-production for both prequels, however, is expected to remain in California, as before.

Because McGregor will also star in both sequels to *Episode I* it guarantees his global fame well into the new millennium, whatever else he does. It is a concept he does not struggle to grasp. 'I haven't considered it 'cos maybe it is too scary to think about.' When tackled as to how he would cope with the film's hype come May 1999, he threw back, 'I'll make sure I'm doing a small independent film up in the back-end of Scotland. It'll have to be somewhere where I can't be reached by phone!' No one doubts that his feet are still well planted on the ground. When invited to consider for a moment what a springboard role Han Solo proved to be for Harrison Ford, McGregor riposted, 'Yeah – look what happened to him. Look what happened to Mark Hamill though!' – a reference to the fact that Hamill hasn't enjoyed the same level of recognition as Ford.

On a more sober note he does admit, 'I knew it was going to be enormous when it came out and I've never been in anything like that before. I wondered how it would juxtapose with the other work I was doing. Some of the actors in the original *Star Wars* didn't do anything else afterwards and I wondered, is that going to happen to me?'

McGregor would not be human if he did not occasionally stop to think that, because everything in his career so far has gone so incredibly well, something dreadful might be lurking round the corner. But it seems very unlikely. The bright-eyed schoolboy determined to become an actor has blazed his way in a dazzlingly short space of time to international popularity. He appeals to men and women alike. In the same short space of time he has established an extraordinary lack of predictability in the range of roles he undertakes. He is in no way hidebound by the question of sustaining an 'attractive' image. 'To not play a weak character because it might make you look weak as a person?' he once queried. 'I would suggest you're not acting, then. Otherwise you'd just end up doing action movies, carrying a machine gun and looking cool all the time. A few actors have done that and made a large amount of money, but I wouldn't suggest they're the best actors in the world.'

His need constantly to expand his horizons found another dimension when he made two brief forays back into the realm of the short. On 1 November 1998, as part of the launch of FilmFour, Channel 4's new subscription television channel, *Desserts* was premiered, a two-minute film written and directed by Jeff Stark in which McGregor was the sole actor. He played a stroller on a deserted beach who discovers a chocolate eclair incongruously sitting on a paper plate on the shore. Picking it up, suspiciously at first, he then bites into it – and pays for yielding to temptation when the eclair proves to be bait and a hook and line snaps out of the mud and reels him into the sea. McGregor revealed, 'It's a film I was faxed while I was making another movie. It arrived on just one sheet of paper and it made me laugh so much I just had to do it. We shot for one day up on the west coast of Scotland and it's quite an interesting little piece of work.'

Then, in January 1999, he would make his directorial debut. The satellite company Sky TV were to make ten separate short films in a series called *Tube Tales* and each story would be set on the London

Underground. McGregor's six-minute tale would be a love story that goes sour. 'I think that being an actor and turning director is a nice growth,' he remarked prior to this new challenge.

Trainspotting director Danny Boyle, who finally moved on to make a film called *The Beach* with *Titanic* heart-throb Leonardo DiCaprio rather than cementing a fourth film with Ewan, still insists, 'Every now and then you come across someone who's a sort of spokesperson for a particular era, someone who sums up a particular feeling or mood. Well, Ewan is one of those people. He is such a contrast to the kind of naked ambition and hardness of the Eighties. He is perfect for this time.' McGregor himself admits, 'I have been incredibly lucky with the amazingly different kinds of people I have worked with. I am enjoying every minute but I do have to pinch myself sometimes.'

If the American film company Miramax had their way, McGregor just might have reached another milestone early in his young life. By late 1998 the Mark Herman directed film *Little Voice*, in addition to attracting three Golden Globe nominations, attracted rave reviews on both sides of the Atlantic, so much so that Miramax quickly made it clear, although Ewan McGregor had missed out on a Golden Globe nomination, that they intended to actively promote McGregor for consideration as a nominee in the Best Supporting Oscar category – for his role as the pigeon-fancying BT engineer Billy – in the 1999 Academy Awards. Alas, it was not to be.

Regardless, Ewan McGregor is already one of the busiest and most successful actors in the business. *Star Wars Episode I: The Phantom Menace* will ensure an explosion of worldwide exposure for McGregor; it will also ensure that he indisputably joins the elite ranks of the most recognisable stars in the galaxy. And, from the evidence thus far, Ewan McGregor is unlikely to stop at that.

Credits

FILM

BEING HUMAN (1993) (USA)

Director: Bill Forsyth
Producer: David Puttnam
Screenplay: Bill Forsyth
Studio: Warner Brothers
Ewan's character: Alvarez
Other cast members: Robin Williams, Hector Elizondo, Jonathan Hyde,
Bill Nighy

SHALLOW GRAVE (1995) (UK)

Director: Danny Boyle
Producer: Andrew Macdonald
Screenplay: John Hodge
Studio: Channel 4/Figment
Ewan's character: Alex Law
Other cast members: Christopher Eccleston, Kerry Fox, Keith Allen,
Ken Stott

BLUE JUICE (1995) (UK)

Director: Carl Prechezer
Producer: Peter Salmi and Simon Relph
Screenplay: Peter Salmi and Carl Prechezer
Studio: Skreba
Ewan's character: Dean Raymond.
Other cast members: Sean Pertwee, Steven Mackintosh, Peter Gunn, Catherine Zeta Jones, Keith Allen

TRAINSPOTTING (1996) (UK)

Director: Danny Boyle
Producer: Andrew Macdonald
Screenplay: John Hodge
Studio: Channel 4/Figment
Ewan's character: Mark Renton
Other cast members: Ewen Bremner, Jonny Lee Miller, Robert Carlyle, Kelly Macdonald, Kevin McKidd, James Cosmo

EMMA (1996) (USA/UK)

Director: Douglas McGrath
Producer: Steven Haft and Patrick Cassavetti
Screenplay: Douglas McGrath
Studio: Miramax
Ewan's character: Frank Churchill
Other cast members: Gwyneth Paltrow, Jeremy Northam, Toni Collette, Alan Cumming, Greta Scacchi, James Cosmo

BRASSED OFF (1996) (UK/USA)

Director: Mark Herman
Producer: Steven Abbott
Screenplay: Mark Herman
Studio: Channel 4/Miramax
Ewan's character: Andy Barrow
Other cast members: Pete Postlethwaite, Stephen Tompkinson,
Tara Fitzgerald, Jim Carter, Peter Gunn, Melanie Hill

THE PILLOW BOOK (1996) (Netherlands/France/UK)

Director: Peter Greenaway
Producer: Kees Kasander
Screenplay: Peter Greenaway
Studio: Kasander & Wigman/Woodline/Alpha/Channel 4
Ewan's character: Jerome
Other cast members: Vivian Wu, Yoshi Oida, Ken Ogata

A LIFE LESS ORDINARY (1997) (UK)

Director: Danny Boyle
Producer: Andrew Macdonald
Screenplay: John Hodge
Studio: Figment
Ewan's character: Robert
Other cast members: Cameron Diaz, Stanley Tucci, Ian Holm,
Holly Hunter, Delroy Lindo

NIGHTWATCH (1998) (USA)

Director: Ole Bornedal
Producer: Michael Obel
Screenplay: Ole Bornedal and Steven Soderbergh
Studio: Miramax
Ewan's character: Martin Belos
Other cast members: Nick Nolte, Patricia Arquette, Josh Brolin

THE SERPENT'S KISS (1998) (UK)

Director: Philippe Rousselot
Producer: Robert Jones, Tim Rose Price, John Battsek
Screenplay: Tim Rose Price
Studio: Trinity Films
Ewan's character: Meneer Chrome
Other cast members: Greta Scacchi, Pete Postlethwaite,
Richard E Grant, Carmen Chaplin

VELVET GOLDMINE (1998) (UK)

Director: Todd Haynes
Producer: Christine Vachon
Screenplay: Todd Haynes
Studio: Channel 4/Zenith
Ewan's character: Curt Wild
Other cast members: Jonathan Rhys Meyers, Christian Bale,
Toni Collette, Eddie Izzard, Emily Woof, Micko Westmoreland

THE RISE AND FALL OF LITTLE VOICE (1998) (USA/UK)

Director: Mark Herman
Producer: Elizabeth Karlsen
Screenplay: Mark Herman
Studio: Miramax/Scala
Ewan's character: Billy
Other cast members: Jane Horrocks, Michael Caine, Brenda Blethyn,
Philip Jackson, Fred Feast

ROGUE TRADER (1999) (UK)

Director: James Dearden
Producer: Paul Raphael, James Dearden
Screenplay: James Dearden
Studio: Granada
Ewan's character: Nick Leeson
Other cast members: Anna Friel, Nigel Lindsey, Lee Ross

EYE OF THE BEHOLDER (1999) (USA)

Director: Stephan Elliott
Producer: Nicolas Clermont, Tony Smith
Screenplay: Stephan Elliott
Studio: MDP Worldwide
Ewan's character: A private detective
Other cast members: Ashley Judd, Patrick Bergen, Genevieve Bujold,
kd lang

STAR WARS EPISODE 1: The Phantom Menace (1999) (USA)

Director: George Lucas
Producer: Rick McCallum
Screenplay: George Lucas
Studio: Lucasfilm
Ewan's character: Obi-Wan Kenobi
Other cast members: Liam Neeson, Ian McDiarmid, Natalie Portman,
Jake Lloyd, Terence Stamp, Brian Blessed, Samuel L Jackson

TELEVISION

LIPSTICK ON YOUR COLLAR (1993)

Channel: Channel 4
Director: Renny Rye
Producer: Rosemarie Whitman
Screenplay: Dennis Potter
Transmission dates: 21 Feburary – 28 March 1993
Ewan's character: Private Mick Hopper
Other cast members: Giles Thomas, Louise Germaine, Douglas Henshall,
Clive Francis, Roy Hudd, Kymberley Huffman

SCARLET AND BLACK (1993)

Channel: BBC
Director: Ben Bolt
Producer: Rosalind Wolfes
Screenplay: Stephen Lowe
Transmission dates: 31 October – 14 November 1993
Ewan's character: Julien Sorel
Other cast members: Rachel Weisz, Alice Krige, Christopher Fulford,
Stratford Johns, T P McKenna, Martin Jarvis, Joseph O'Conor

DOGGIN' AROUND (1994)

Channel: BBC
Director: Desmond Davis
Producer: Otto Plaschkes
Screenplay: Alan Plater
Transmission date: 16 October 1994
Ewan's character: Tom Clayton
Other cast members: Elliott Gould, Geraldine James, Liz Smith,
Alun Armstrong

KAVANAGH QC: Nothing But The Truth (1995)

Channel: ITV (Carlton)
Director: Colin Gregg
Producer: Chris Kelly
Screenplay: Russell Lewis
Transmission date: 3 January 1995
Ewan's character: David Armstrong
Other cast members: John Thaw, Geraldine James, Alison Steadman,
Daisy Bates

KARAOKE (1996)

Channel: BBC
Director: Renny Rye
Producer: Kenith Trodd, Rosemarie Whitman
Screenplay: Dennis Potter
Transmission date: 28 April 1996
Ewan's character: Walk-on, unnamed.
Other cast members: Albert Finney, Roy Hudd, Julie Christie

ER: The Long Way Around (1997)

Channel: NBC, USA
Director: Christopher Chulack
Producer: Christopher Chulack
Screenplay: Lydia Woodward
Transmission date: In UK 13 April 1997
Ewan's character: Duncan Stewart
Other cast members: George Clooney, Julianna Margulies

THEATRE

WHAT THE BUTLER SAW (1993)

Theatre: Salisbury Playhouse
Director: Penny Ciniewicz
Writer: Joe Orton
Run: January/February 1993
Ewan's character: Nicholas Beckett
Other cast members: Isla Blair, Roger Sloman, Paul Viragh,
Jeremy Child, Jacqueline Defferary

LITTLE MALCOM AND HIS STRUGGLE AGAINST THE EUNUCHS (November 1998–February 1999)

Theatre: Hampstead Theatre Club
Director: Denis Lawson
Writer: David Halliwell
Run: November 1998–January 1999
Ewan's character: Malcolm Scrawdyke
Other cast members: Joe Duttine, Sean Gilder, Nicolas Tenrant, Lou Gish

Ewan also appeared in the following short films:
Family Style (1994)
Swimming With The Fishes (1996)
Desserts (1998)

He took part in the following BBC radio plays:
Tragic Prelude (1992)
The Real Thing (1992)

Picture Credits

Cover image © Rex Features

First Plate Section

1. Courtesy of Bob Stewart
2. Courtesy of Grampian Television
3. Rex Features
4. Polygram/Pictorial Press Ltd
5. Polygram/Pictorial Press Ltd
6. Rex Features
7. Rex Features

Second Plate Section

1. Polygram/Pictorial Press Ltd
2. Polygram/Pictorial Press Ltd
3. Polygram/Pictorial Press Ltd
4. Rex Features
5. Polygram/Pictorial Press Ltd
6. Polygram/Pictorial Press Ltd
7. Rex Features
8. Kasander & Wigman/Alpha Films (courtesy Kobal)

Third Plate Section

1. Courtesy of the Grimethorpe Colliery Band
2. Rex Features
3. Universal Pictorial Ltd
4. Andrew Milligan, Newsflash Scotland
5. Rex Features
6. Tim O'Sullivan/The Sunday Times, London

Fourth Plate Section

1. Polygram/Pictorial Press Ltd
2. Rex Features
3. Pictorial Press Ltd
4. Rex Features
5. All Action
6. Popperfoto
7. Andrew Milligan, Newsflash Scotland

Index